To Lois –

Happy Ne~

Kosher cooking

Love –
Kathy

July 10, 1980

Dorothy Seaman & Paula Smith's

NOT CHOPPED LIVER!

THE KOSHER WAY TO COOK GOURMET

JETSAND
PRESS

Library of Congress Catalog Card Number: 78-71124

ISBN 0-933374-00-3

Published in the United States by

Jetsand Press

Box 17052

West Hartford, Connecticut 06117

contents

All ingredients listed are by nature kosher, and all are available free of dairy derivitives. The regular rules of kashering apply to all meats and poultry. Any recipe containing fish can be served separately and before the main dish.

Consult the **Code of Jewish Law** for the rules governing kashruth. Questions are traditionally brought to the Rabbinical authorities for clarification.

Each recipe will serve six to eight persons, unless otherwise indicated.

Foreword

This book is designed for the *fleishig* or meat table only, and any recipe in this book can be served in combination with all other recipes in this book. The traditional Jewish homemaker now has a recipe reference book that can be called upon when planning a meat menu, the area which presents the most problems to the Jewish cook who attempts to prepare tasty attractive gourmet meals. One is now able to introduce into one's repertoire, recipes from all the great cuisines of the world.

In this book are found French, Italian, Viennese, Indian and Chinese recipes . . . gourmet recipes which can all be served in the kosher home. Also included in good number are the "throw-together" recipes that are the main-stay of every busy homemaker's recipe collection.

Products that are available to us in today's market-place and are free of dairy derivitives have been used. We have also used foodstuffs available in natural food stores, products made and produced in Israel, and a variety of smoked meats available at the local delicatessen. By using these commodities and by altering and accommodating original ingredients in classical recipes, we have developed the recipes in this book.

We realize that to the uninitiated there is a complete mystique surrounding kosher cooking and, certainly, Jewish stand-up comics always elicit a laugh when describing the ethnic cooking they consumed while growing up. The recipes in this book would pass the test of taste and quality in the finest restaurants.

This book should encourage the homemaker who is deliberating the decision of keeping a kosher home and will answer the questions she is asking herself: "Will I be able to present a beautiful table — one that will allow me to be an equal with my peers? Can I cook on a regular basis, day in, day out, presenting tasty food, varied and interesting, food high in quality and food that I shall enjoy preparing?"

This book will provide support and a source of help to the committed, yet inexperienced, kosher homemaker. This book will certainly add zest, fun and a new eagerness to the established kosher cook.

It is to these ends that we have dedicated ourselves while preparing this book. For we firmly believe that one of the most positive things one can do to preserve and promote Judaism in the home, is to keep a traditional kosher home reflecting warmth, love and the desire to perpetuate the tenets of Judaism.

FIRST COURSES

steak tartare

  1 lb. boneless rib eye steak
  ½ C scallions
  1 egg yolk
  ¼ t salt
  ½ t pepper
  1 t capers
  4 egg yolks, unbroken
     chopped onion
     capers
     chopped parsley

1. Trim the meat well of all fat. Combine the first 6 ingredients and process or grind twice.
2. Form into 4 patties. Place an egg yolk on each patty.
3. Serve with garnishes of onion, capers and parsley.

Tiny balls may be formed instead of patties. Dip into egg white and then into chopped walnuts and serve on picks.

curried beef turnovers

  ½ lb. ground beef
  1 onion, minced
     cooking oil
  1 T soy sauce
  ½ t sugar
  2 t curry powder
  1 recipe Flaky Pastry

1. Saute beef and onion in cooking oil for 2 minutes.
2. Add soy sauce, sugar and stir well.
3. Add curry powder, mix well and cook an additional 2 minutes. Cool.
4. Roll out pastry dough and cut into circles. Place 1 teaspoon of beef mixture in circle. Fold in half and seal edges with a fork. Place on cookie sheet.
5. Bake in a 400° oven for 40 minutes or until brown.

saucey cocktail meatballs

1 lb. ground beef
2 T bread crumbs
1 egg
½ t salt
½ C green pepper, minced
½ C onion, minced
2 T margarine
10 oz. can tomato soup
2 T brown sugar
4 t Worcestershire sauce
1 T dry mustard
1 T vinegar

1. Mix beef, bread crumbs, egg and salt together. Shape into 50 balls.

2. Place in a shallow baking pan and broil until brown on all sides. Remove all fat.

3. In saucepan, cook pepper and onion in margarine until tender. Stir in remaining ingredients.

4. Pour this sauce over the meatballs. Cover and bake in a 350° oven for 20 minutes.

Cocktail franks may be substituted for the meatballs; or use a combination of franks and meatballs.

wurst vessels

½ of a midget salami
2 oz. tofu
½ t garlic salt
1 egg yolk
   green stuffed olives, sliced

1. Slice the salami into 15 round pieces by cutting straight down; do not elongate slice by cutting on a diagonal.

2. Broil the salami slices until they form cup shapes. Drain on paper towels. Remove to cookie sheet.

3. Blend together the tofu, garlic salt and egg yolk.

4. Place a spoonful of tofu mixture in each salami cup.

5. Return to broiler until filling is hot and lightly browned.

6. Garnish with green olive slices; serve hot.

A midget salami weighs about 12 ounces and is about one and one half inches in diameter. It yields a perfect bite sized pick-up.

tongue spread

1 C cold smoked tongue
1 T gherkins
1 T chives
1 hard cooked egg
1 t prepared mustard
1½ T mayonnaise
   snack crackers

1. Grind first 4 ingredients together.

2. Add mustard and mayonnaise.

3. Spread on your favorite snack cracker.

nutty chili dogs

frankfurters
¼ C peanut butter
4 T prepared mustard
½ C chili sauce
toast rounds

1. Prepare frankfurters by slicing 3 V-shaped channels lengthwise into the sides. Slice scored frankfurters into thin pieces, creating fluted rounds.

2. Combine peanut butter, mustard and chili sauce. Heat until melted; stir until blended. Cool.

3. Spread toast rounds with the cooled mixture.

4. Top each round with a slice of frankfurter.

5. Place under broiler until heated through.

Use your imagination: create diamonds, squares, triangles, etc. from the frankfurters. Cut the toast into odd shapes with cookie cutters or a sharp knife.

croque monsieur

4 T tehina
4 T tofu
12 thin slices challah, trimmed
6 slices smoked dark meat turkey
2 eggs mixed with 2 t water
margarine

1. Mash tehina and tofu together.

2. Layer as follows to make 6 sandwiches:
   1 slice of bread spread with tofu mixture
   1 slice of smoked dark meat turkey
   1 slice of bread spread with tofu mixture (tofu mixture side down)

3. Dip each sandwich into the egg mixture.

4. Fry in margarine on both sides until golden brown.

This is a very hearty appetizer. It can readily serve as an entree for luncheon.

chick sticks

   1 C cooked chicken
   2 T chives
   1 T parsley
   ¼ C celery
   1 slice bread
   1 T onion
   1 t curry powder
   1 T Dijon style mustard
   1 egg beaten with 1 T water
      bread crumbs
      cooking oil

1. Grind together the chicken, chives, parsley, celery, bread and onion.

2. Mix in the curry powder and mustard. Form into balls.

3. Dip into egg mixture and then into bread crumbs. Refrigerate overnight.

4. Deep-fry in 375° oil until golden. Drain.

5. Serve immediately on party picks.

chicken pate

   2½ C cooked chicken
    1 celery stalk
    1 T green pepper
    2 onions
    2 green olives, pitted
    ½ C mayonnaise
    ¼ t celery salt
    ¼ t white pepper
    1 t parsley, minced

1. Grind together the chicken, celery, green pepper, onions and green olives.

2. Blend in the mayonnaise, celery salt, pepper and parsley.

3. Refrigerate overnight. Remove from refrigerator and allow to reach room temperature before serving.

Cooked turkey may be substituted for the chicken.

stuffed mushrooms

12 large mushrooms
4 T margarine, melted
¼ t salt
¼ t white pepper
2 T shallots, minced
1½ t flour
½ C liquid non-dairy creamer
3 T parsley, minced

1. Remove the stems from the mushrooms and reserve. Set aside caps.

2. Mince the stems. Place them in a clean dish towel and press out the excess water.

3. Dip outsides of caps into melted margarine. Sprinkle insides with salt and pepper. Place in a shallow baking dish.

4. Saute shallots and stems in remaining margarine until limp. Remove from heat.

5. Sprinkle in flour and mix well. Pour in non-dairy creamer.

6. Place over low heat and stir until thickened. Add parsley.

7. Fill caps with mixture. Bake in a 375° oven for 15 minutes.

These mushrooms serve equally well as a side dish or as a garnish.

oeufs farcis I

3 hard cooked eggs
4 oz. mushrooms, minced
2 shallots, minced
1 T cooking oil
   mayonnaise

1. Cut eggs in half. Gently remove yolks and mash.

2. Saute mushrooms and shallots in cooking oil until tender. Cool.

3. Combine mushrooms and shallots with the egg yolks. Mash all together. Add enough mayonnaise to hold mixture together.

4. Spoon or pipe egg yolk mixture into egg whites.

Each stuffed egg has a distinctive flavor, and certainly a color of its own. Use these to add interest, and to garnish, any hors d'oeuvre platter.

oeufs farcis II

3 hard cooked eggs
4 oz. frozen peas
   mayonnaise

1. Cut eggs in half. Gently remove yolks and mash.

2. Cook peas in boiling water until very tender. Remove and drain well. Puree in food processor or put through a sieve.

3. Combine peas with the egg yolks. Mash all together. Add enough mayonnaise to hold mixture together.

4. Spoon or pipe egg yolk mixture into egg whites.

eggs a la russe

4 hard cooked eggs
1 C mayonnaise
3 T chili sauce
1 t pimento, minced
1 t chives, minced

1. Slice eggs in half and place yolk side down.

2. Combine remaining ingredients.

3. Spoon sauce over the eggs.

antipasto

Marinated vegetables, served in combination with salami cornucopias and stuffed eggs, form a delicious cold antipasto, (assorted appetizer tray), which is often served as a first course at an Italian dinner. The following nine recipes can be served in any combination.

Of course, it is always appropriate to serve a single marinated vegetable as a first course. Call upon the many types of lettuce available, and arrange interesting combinations of vegetables on lettuce leaves; play textures and colors against each other.

caponato

1   lb. eggplant, cut into ½'' cubes
4   T olive oil
1   C celery, chopped
½   C onions, chopped
3   T wine vinegar
2   t sugar
1½ C canned Italian plum tomatoes, drained
1   T tomato sauce
3   large green olives, pitted, slivered, rinsed
1   T capers
1   t salt
¼   t black pepper
2   T pine nuts

1. In 2 tablespoon olive oil, saute celery and onions for 20 minutes. Remove from skillet and reserve.

2. In same pan, add remaining olive oil and saute eggplant 8 minutes. Return celery and onions to skillet. Add vinegar, sugar, tomatoes, tomato paste, green olives, capers, salt and pepper. Bring to a boil; reduce heat and simmer, uncovered, for 15 minutes.

3. Stir in pine nuts. Chill.

black olives

6 oz. can ripe olives, pitted
¼ t crushed red pepper
2 cloves garlic, crushed
3 sprigs dill
3 T olive oil

1. Drain olives and reserve liquid.
2. Add remaining ingredients to olives in glass bowl.
3. Add enough of the reserved liquid to cover olives.
4. Marinate for three days. Strain and serve.

green olives

8 oz. green Italian olives
3 cloves garlic, crushed
½ t crushed red pepper
2 sprigs dill
1 bay leaf
¼ C olive oil
¼ C vinegar

1. Crush the olives until they split, but do not break apart.
2. Combine all ingredients. Marinate for three days.
3. Drain and serve.

asparagus

2 pkgs. frozen asparagus, thawed, drained
⅓ C sugar
¾ C vinegar
¾ C water
3 T corn oil
½ t salt
1 t pickling spice
1 clove garlic
1 onion, sliced thin

1. Bring sugar, vinegar, water, oil, salt and pickling spice to a boil. Add garlic.

2. Layer asparagus and onions in a glass bowl. Pour the marinade over.

3. Cover and refrigerate for three days. Strain and serve.

carrots

1 C white wine
1 C chicken broth
5 T olive oil
3 T red wine vinegar
2 shallots, chopped
1 clove garlic, minced
1 t salt
1 t sugar
¼ t white pepper
¼ t thyme
1 T parsley, chopped
1 bay leaf
12 oz. crinkle cut frozen carrots, thawed, drained
15 walnut halves, blanched

1. Bring first 12 ingredients to a boil and cook for 2 minutes.

2. Combine marinade and carrots.

3. Marinate overnight. Strain. Toss with nuts before serving.

Lemon slices can be used to garnish this unique dish.

mushrooms

⅔ C tarragon vinegar
½ C corn oil
1 clove garlic, minced
1 T sugar
1½ t salt
⅛ t pepper
2 T water
⅛ t hot pepper sauce
1 onion, sliced into rings
12 oz. small, uniform mushroom
   caps

1. Combine first 8 ingredients. Add onions and mushrooms.

2. Cover and refrigerate overnight. Drain and serve.

zucchini

4 C zucchini, diced
½ C salad oil
¼ C vinegar
1 envelope dry spaghetti sauce mix,
   or chili sauce mix
1 t sugar
1 green pepper, chopped
1 onion, chopped

1. Mix all ingredients together. Refrigerate overnight.

2. Drain and serve.

stuffed eggs

6 hard cooked eggs
¼ C mayonnaise
¼ t dry mustard
½ t salt
⅛ t pepper
2 T parsley, minced
2 T chives, minced
   paprika

1. Cut eggs in half. Gently remove yolks and mash.

2. Blend together yolks and remaining ingredients.

3. Spoon or pipe egg yolk mixture into egg whites. Garnish with paprika.

garbanzo relish

1 lb. 4 oz. can chick peas, drained
1 onion, chopped
1 T oregano
3 T oil
2 T vinegar
1 t sugar
¼ t black pepper

Mix all ingredients together and refrigerate overnight.

chick pea spread

- 1 clove garlic
- ½ C lemon juice
- 3 T water
- ¼ C olive oil
- ½ t salt
- 1 lb. 4 oz. can chick peas, drained
  pita bread

Blend together first 6 ingredients in a blender or food processor. Spread on pita bread, or your favorite snack cracker.

artichoke hearts with garlic

- 8½ oz. can artichoke hearts, drained
  garlic snack crackers
- ¼ C margarine, melted
- 1 clove garlic
- ½ t salt
- ½ t pepper
- 1 T sesame seeds

1. Cut artichoke hearts into quarters. Arrange crackers on a cookie sheet. Place 1 piece of artichoke heart on a cracker.

2. Mash garlic clove and salt together to form a paste.

3. Combine margarine, garlic paste, pepper and sesame seeds.

4. Pour a little of this sauce over each artichoke.

5. Bake in a 350° oven for 5 minutes. Place under broiler for 2 minutes. Serve hot.

creamy garlic rounds

4 oz. tofu
½ clove garlic
1 egg yolk
4 oz. can chopped mushrooms
  garlic snack crackers

1. Place the tofu, garlic and egg yolk in a blender and puree.

2. Drain the mushrooms on paper towels. Gently stir into tofu mixture.

3. Place snack crackers on cookie sheet. Top each cracker with some mushroom mixture.

4. Broil for 5 minutes or until hot and lightly browned.

skinny potatoes

shells from baked potatoes
softened margarine
salt
pepper

1. Scrape all potato meat from potato skins.

2. Spread margarine on both sides of potato skins. Sprinkle with salt and pepper. Cut into strips.

3. Broil until crisp.

spinach roll

2　pkgs. frozen chopped spinach, thawed, squeezed
15　oz. can artichokes, pureed
⅛　t pepper
½　t salt
¼　t nutmeg
6　T margarine, melted
5　egg yolks
5　egg whites, beaten stiff
1　recipe Chicken Filling

1. Mix spinach and artichokes with salt, pepper, nutmeg, margarine and egg yolks.

2. Fold in egg whites.

3. Grease jelly roll pan. Line with wax paper and grease again.

4. Pour spinach mixture into prepared pan. Bake in a 375° oven for 18 minutes.

5. Flop over onto a clean dish towel and allow to stand 5 minutes.

6. Peel off wax paper and roll up while hot. Unroll and spread with **Chicken Filling.** Reroll; slice into serving pieces.

chicken filling

1　C cooked chicken, chopped
2　T margarine
2　T flour
1　C liquid non-dairy creamer
½　t salt
½　t pepper
⅛　t nutmeg

1. Melt margarine; stir in flour and cook for 2 minutes, stirring constantly. Gradually add non-dairy creamer and cook until thick.

2. Add chicken and seasonings.

melanzana con melone

eggplant with melon

> 2 lbs. eggplant
> ¼ C cooking oil
> ¼ t salt
> 1 ripe cantaloupe

1. Cut unpeeled eggplant into 1 inch cubes.

2. Saute the eggplant in cooking oil until just tender. The eggplant must retain its shape and not become too soft.

3. Remove, toss with salt, and cool to room temperature.

4. Cut the meat of the melon into 1 inch cubes.

5. Combine the melon and eggplant and serve.

In northern Italy, many Jewish homemakers serve this dish instead of prosciutto and melon.

citrus cup

> ½ C honey
> ½ C water
> ⅓ C cider vinegar
> 3 T rum
> 1 T onion, minced
> 1 T rosemary
> 1 t soy sauce
> 2 C citrus fruit sections

Bring all ingredients, except fruit, to a boil. Pour over fruit and marinate overnight.

Use oranges, tangerines or grapefruit sections in any or all combinations.

guacamole

2　very ripe avocados
1　t onion juice
¼　t hot sauce
1　t lemon juice
½　t salt
¼　t pepper

1. Remove stone from avocados and re-serve.
2. Mash avocado meat with a fork. Mix in remaining ingredients.
3. Place stone into mixture. Refrigerate.
4. Remove stone just before serving.

This highly seasoned dip is very popular in Spanish speaking countries. It is best served with corn chips.

tomatoes 'n stuff

24　cherry tomatoes
2　C potato chips
½　C imitation-bacon flavored bits
½　C mayonnaise

1. Cut the stem end off the tomatoes. Squeeze them gently to remove seeds and pulp. Invert and drain.
2. Crush potato chips. Mix together with the imitation-bacon flavored bits. Add the mayonnaise to bind the mixture together.
3. Fill tomatoes with this mixture. Chill and serve.

Brightly colored red tomatoes always lend more than just flavor to an hors d'oeuvre platter.

cornets de saumon fume

lox cornucopias

16 slices smoked Nova Scotia salmon
1 lb. cod, cooked, cooled
¼ recipe Chaud-Froid Sauce
made with fish stock
½ t salt
½ t white pepper

1. Roll the slices of salmon to form cones.
2. Blend the remaining ingredients together.
3. Fill the cones and chill for 2 hours before serving.

This dish makes a very attractive appetizer and can be garnished quite handsomely with lemon slices, chopped parsley and capers. It serves well as an elegant first course on a French dinner menu.

creamy lox canapes

¼ lb. smoked Nova Scotia salmon
1 oz. tofu
2 t onion
2 t liquid non-dairy creamer
½ t lemon juice
¼ t dill
¼ t pepper
party rye bread, sliced thin
tomato, sliced
onion, sliced thin
capers

1. Blend together the salmon, tofu, onion, non-dairy creamer, lemon juice, dill and pepper.
2. Layer party bread with a slice of tomato and a slice of onion. Pipe a rosette of pureed salmon mixture on each round and top with a caper.

This, of course, looks like a lox and cream cheese spread.

fish tartlets

1 recipe Flaky Pastry
2 onions, chopped
¼ C margarine
2 t curry powder
1 T chutney
1 T golden raisins, chopped
1 T shredded, unsweetened coconut
½ C almonds, chopped
1 C liquid non-dairy creamer
2 T cornstarch, dissolved in 2 T cold
    water
1 C fish, cooked, flaked
    (scrod, sole or flounder)

1. Place pastry in individual tartlet shells; bake as directed.

2. Saute onions in margarine until limp. Add curry powder and cook 1 minute. Add chutney, raisins, coconut, almonds and non-dairy creamer.

3. Add cornstarch mixture and cook until thickened. Remove from heat and add fish. Cool.

4. Spoon mixture into tartlet shells. Place under the broiler to brown lightly.

Please note that the coconut is unsweetened and not the baking variety. It can usually be purchased in natural food stores.

tuna vegetable dip

2 T lemon juice
6½ oz. can light tuna in olive oil, drained
7 anchovy fillets
2 T capers
2 C mayonnaise

1. Blend together all ingredients in a blender or food processor. Chill.
2. Serve with an assortment of raw vegetables.

Suggested vegetables: mushrooms, cauliflower, carrots, peppers, celery, radishes, zucchini.

sardine puffs

3¾ oz. can sardines, drained, mashed
⅔ C mayonnaise
2 egg whites, beaten stiff
toast rounds

1. Mix mayonnaise and mashed sardines together.
2. Fold into beaten egg whites.
3. Place dollops of mixture on toast rounds. Place under broiler and cook until hot and puffy.

tofu in carrozza

20 slices challah
10 thin slices tofu
    tehina
 ¾ C liquid non-dairy creamer
    bread crumbs
  2 eggs mixed with 2 T liquid
        non-dairy creamer
    cooking oil

For an interesting effect, cut bread and tofu with cookie cutters.

This Neapolitan dish is served as an hors d'oeuvre; the sandwiches may be topped with a warm **Anchovy Sauce.**

1. Cut bread to the same size as the tofu.

2. Layer as follows to make 10 sandwiches:
    1 slice of bread spread with tehina
    1 slice of tofu
    1 slice of bread spread with tehina,
        (tehina side down)

3. Dip each sandwich in liquid non-dairy creamer.

4. Dip all sides of sandwich in bread crumbs.

5. Dip in egg mixture.

6. Fry in cooking oil on all sides until golden brown.

7. Drain and serve hot.

anchovy sauce

8 T margarine
4 anchovy fillets
1 T parsley, minced
2 t capers, minced
2 t lemon juice

Combine all ingredients. Heat until anchovies are dissolved.

fior di zucchine
squash blossoms

> 18 zucchini flowers (male blossoms only)
> 2 eggs
> 1½ T olive oil
> ⅔ C warm water
> ¾ C flour
> 2 oz. can anchovy fillets, drained, chopped
> cooking oil

1. Mix eggs, oil and water. Beat in flour. This mixture should be the consistency of pancake batter. Set aside.

2. Gently remove pistils from flowers. Wash and dry flowers.

3. Place a small bit of anchovy in each flower.

4. Dip in batter and fry in cooking oil on all sides until golden.

We are sorry to say that blossoms are not usually sold in markets. You must raise your own. This is a very special recipe for gardeners and their friends.

scarola con bagna cauda
escarole with hot dressing

> 1 head escarole
> 2 oz. can anchovies, drained
> 1 clove garlic, minced
> 3 T olive oil
> 3 T red wine vinegar

1. Tear escarole into bite size pieces.

2. Saute garlic in olive oil.

3. Add anchovy fillets and cook until anchovies dissolve.

4. Stir in vinegar and heat until bubbles form.

5. Pour this hot dressing over escarole; toss gently and serve this salad immediately.

This dressing is very strongly flavored.

broccoli salad

1 lb. broccoli, cooked, chopped
2 oz. can anchovies, drained, chopped
¼ lb. Greek olives
½ t capers
2 T lemon juice
⅛ t crushed red pepper
3 T olive oil
1 lemon, sliced thin

1. Combine broccoli, anchovies, olives, and capers.
2. Combine lemon juice, crushed red pepper and oil.
3. Combine two mixtures and toss together.
4. Garnish with lemon slices; serve.

brutus salad

1 head romaine lettuce
1 clove garlic
½ C olive oil
½ t salt
½ t pepper
1 egg, coddled
¼ C lemon juice
2 oz. can anchovies, drained
1 C croutons

1. Tear lettuce into bite size pieces; refrigerate.
2. Add garlic to oil and allow to stand at room temperature for 2 hours. Discard garlic.
3. Add ingredients to lettuce in following order and toss after each addition: salt, pepper, oil, egg, lemon juice, anchovies and croutons.

basic cream of vegetable soup

1 C cooked vegetables, or 1 pkg. frozen vegetables, thawed, drained
1½ C liquid non-dairy creamer
3 T margarine
2 T flour
1 t salt
¼ t pepper
1 t Worcestershire sauce
1 T sherry
¼ t nutmeg

1. Puree all ingredients together in a blender.
2. Heat until very warm. Serve with **Herbed Toast Fingers.**

Suggested vegetables are: broccoli, asparagus, corn, cauliflower, lima beans, and green beans.

herbed toast fingers

¾ C margarine
¼ t thyme
½ t salt
½ t pepper
1 T lemon juice
1 t parsley, chopped
1 clove garlic, minced
1 shallot, minced
12 slices white bread, trimmed, cut into fingers

1. Combine all ingredients, except bread, and heat until margarine is melted.
2. Dip bread into herb mixture and place on baking sheet.
3. Bake in a 350° oven for 10 minutes.
4. Turn and brown the other side.
5. Serve hot, warm or at room temperature.

creme crecy

cream of carrot soup

          1 lb. pkg. frozen carrots
          2 onions, halved
          1 bay leaf
       3½ C chicken broth
          2 C liquid non-dairy creamer
          ½ t salt
          ½ t pepper
          ¼ C cooked rice
          2 T sherry

1. Boil carrots, onions and bay leaf in chicken broth until tender. Puree in blender or food processor.

2. Heat liquid non-dairy creamer to just below the boiling point. Add to warm pureed carrot mixture. Add seasonings.

3. Add rice and sherry. Serve.

zucchini soup

          2 lbs. zucchini, chopped
          ½ onion, chopped
          3 C chicken broth
       1½ t curry powder
          ½ t salt
          ¼ t pepper
       1½ C liquid non-dairy creamer
          ¼ C sherry
             chopped chives

1. Cook the zucchini, onions and dry seasonings in the chicken broth until the zucchini is tender.

2. Process in blender.

3. Add non-dairy creamer and sherry.

4. Chill. Garnish with chives, and serve.

risi e bisi
rice and peas

  1 onion, chopped
  4 T margarine
1½ C rice, uncooked
3½ C chicken broth
1½ t salt
  ½ t pepper
  1 pkg. frozen green peas, thawed

1. Saute onion in margarine until transparent. Add rice and saute until rice is transparent.

2. Add the broth, salt and pepper. Bring to a boil and simmer slowly for 15 minutes, or until rice is cooked.

3. Add peas and cook until peas are heated through.

This thick rice dish is traditionally served as a soup course in Northern Italy.

french pea soup

  ½ C onion, chopped
  ¼ t mint
  1 T margarine
1¼ C chicken broth
  1 pkg. frozen peas, thawed
  ¼ t salt
  ¼ t pepper
1½ C liquid non-dairy creamer

1. Saute onion and mint in margarine until onion is soft and translucent.

2. Add broth, peas, salt and pepper. Heat to boiling. Cover, reduce heat and cook 8 minutes.

3. Process in blender until smooth. Add liquid non-dairy creamer.

4. Chill and serve.

Thinly sliced cucumbers, sprinkled with chopped chives, make an attractive garnish for this summer pea soup.

curried tomato soup

    4 C tomato juice
    1 t curry powder
    3 T tomato paste
    1 t salt
    ½ t basil
    ¼ t pepper
    1 C liquid non-dairy creamer
    3 T lemon juice

1. Stir curry powder into tomato juice; simmer 10 minutes.

2. Add tomato paste, salt, basil and pepper. Stir to dissolve paste; bring to a boil.

3. Add liquid non-dairy creamer and lemon juice.

4. Chill. Garnish with chives, and serve.

chilly dilly soup

    1 lb. canned tomatoes
    1 T tomato paste
    5 sprigs fresh dill
    ¼ t salt
    ¼ t pepper
    ¼ t garlic salt
    1 C chicken broth
    ½ C cooked macaroni
    ¾ C liquid non-dairy creamer
    ¼ C sherry

1. Simmer the tomatoes, tomato paste and seasonings in the chicken broth for 15 minutes.

2. Add remaining ingredients and process in blender.

3. Chill and serve.

bittersweet summer soup

2 C orange juice
2 C tomato juice
2 T lemon juice
½ t basil
¼ t white pepper
¼ t salt
  dash cayenne pepper

1. Combine all ingredients.
2. Chill and serve.

melon soup

2 C cantaloupe, cubed
2 T margarine
1½ C chicken broth
1 C liquid non-dairy creamer
½ t ginger
  mint leaves

1. Saute melon in margarine for 8 minutes.
2. Add chicken broth and bring to a boil. Reduce heat and simmer 15 minutes.
3. Puree this mixture in a blender or food processor. Add non-dairy creamer and ginger. Heat until hot.
4. Serve garnished with mint.

gazpacho

3 slices white bread, trimmed
¼ C red wine vinegar
6 tomatoes
½ green pepper
1 cucumber
½ clove garlic
½ onion
½ t salt
3 T water
½ C olive oil
½ t pepper

garnitures:
   chopped cucumber
   diced green pepper
   chopped parsley
   thinly sliced scallions
   garlic croutons

1. Soak bread in vinegar.
2. Place all ingredients, except oil, in a blender and blend until smooth.
3. With blender on, slowly add oil. Chill.
4. Serve cold with an assortment of any or all of the garnitures.

There are as many recipes for Gazpacho as there are for chicken soup.

spanish soup

1¼ C almonds, blanched
4 slices white bread, trimmed
⅓ C white wine vinegar
2 cloves garlic
4 C ice water
⅔ C olive oil
seedless grapes, peeled

1. Puree all ingredients, except grapes, in food processor or blender.
2. Chill; add grapes as a garnish and serve.

peanut butter soup

3 T onion, minced
1 T margarine
2 T flour
1 C peanut butter, creamy or chunky-style
4 C chicken broth
¼ t white pepper
1 C liquid non-dairy creamer
salted peanuts, chopped

1. Saute onion in margarine until limp. Stir in flour and cook 2 minutes.
2. Add peanut butter and stir until melted.
3. Add chicken broth and pepper. Simmer uncovered for 20 minutes.
4. Add liquid non-dairy creamer. Heat through and serve hot, garnished with peanuts.

MAIN DISHES

roast prime ribs of beef

Contrary to popular opinion, roasting a rib of beef to perfection is a true culinary skill. As always, experience is the best teacher, but do take all possible steps to avoid a disaster with this most expensive cut of beef. If you will be consistant in your preparation, you will soon be able to time your roast accurately.

One should not prepare a standing rib roast of less than three ribs. (The bigger the better is a truism.)

Have the butcher prepare the roast by cutting off the short ribs. Reserve these for another dish. Allow the roast to reach room temperature. Place the roast on a rack, rib side down. Insert a meat thermometer into the center of the rib, through the top. The depth of the tip of the thermometer should reach the center of the roast. It is essential to use a meat thermometer because there are so many variables: the size of the roast, the amount of bone, and the proportion of lean to fat, all effect the cooking time.

Place the roast in a preheated oven. We suggest a constant 325° as the proper temperature for roasting a standing rib. This is a non-searing method of roasting meat, and we recommend it for less shrinkage. Do not cover the meat, do not add any liquid to the pan and do not baste the meat.

As a guide, for a four rib roast, figure approximately 20 minutes to the pound for a rare roast, 25 minutes to the pound for medium, and 30 minutes to the pound for well done. Again, let us emphasize that there are many variables to consider.

Allow the roast to rest at least 15 minutes after it is removed from the oven. (Rare meat lovers take note: a slight cooking process does continue during this time.) This allows most of the juice to remain in the slice and facilitates carving.

beef wellington

boneless rib eye roast, trimmed
   of all fat
1 lb. mushrooms, minced
6 shallots, minced
4 T margarine
2 T parsley, minced
6 chicken livers, broiled
2 T brandy
1 recipe Flaky Pastry
1 egg yolk beaten with 1 T water

1. Place meat on rack in open roasting pan and roast in a 400° oven until desired state of doneness. Set aside. Meat must be at room temperature to assemble.

2. Saute the mushrooms and shallots in the margarine until the wetness disappears. Add parsley and cook an additional 2 minutes. Set aside this duxelles.

3. Prepare liver by blending chicken livers and brandy into a very smooth consistency. Set aside.

4. Roll pastry ⅛ inch thick to a size that will completely encompass the fillet of beef.

5. Place beef in center of dough. Spread the liver over the beef. Pat on the duxelles.

6. Seal the meat completely in the pastry, using cold water along the seams. Slash to create a vent. Use left-over pastry dough for decorative applique; apply with cold water.

7. Brush with egg wash. Bake in a 450° oven for 20 minutes, or until the pastry is golden brown.

All parts should be at room temperature when assembled.

stuffed oven roast

2 lb. shoulder roast

3 onions, diced

4 T cooking oil

2 cloves garlic, minced

18 black olives, pitted, chopped

½ C smoked dark meat turkey,
   chopped

1 t thyme

2 T parsley, chopped

1 egg yolk, beaten

1. Slice horizontally almost through the meat, thus creating a pocket.

2. Saute the onions in the cooking oil until limp. Add garlic, olives, turkey, thyme and parsley. Stir until well blended.

3. Stir in the egg yolk and cook 2 minutes. Remove from heat.

4. Stuff this mixture into the pocket which has been created in the meat.

5. Place the meat on a rack; roast in a 325° degree oven for 1½ hours.

Choose an oven dish to accompany the roast. One can't be too energy conscious.

roast beef sandwich

2 C leftover roast beef, diced
½ C onion, chopped
2 cloves garlic, minced
4 T margarine
¼ C parsley
1 slice ginger root
⅛ t cloves
⅛ t nutmeg
   pinch cayenne pepper
⅛ t salt
⅛ t pepper
4 slices rye bread
   onion rings

1. Saute onion, and garlic in margarine until limp.
2. Add the roast beef, parsley and ginger root. Cook for 5 minutes.
3. Grind this mixture together. Add seasonings.
4. Spread on the bread and place under the broiler for 4 minutes.
5. Top with onion rings.

horseradish sauce for roast beef

¼ C prepared white horseradish, drained
1 t sugar
1 t white wine vinegar
½ t salt
1 C mayonnaise
2 t mustard
½ C non-dairy whipping cream, whipped

Combine all ingredients.

bifteck saute sans beurre

4 boneless rib eye steaks, cut
½'' thick
margarine
½ C dry red wine
1 T margarine, softened

1. Heat enough margarine to film the bottom of a frying pan.

2. Add steaks to pan and cook over high heat for about 4 minutes.

3. Turn the steaks with tongs and cook to desired state of doneness. Remove to a warm serving platter.

4. Pour off excess grease from pan. Return pan to heat; deglaze with wine.

5. Add softened margarine and swirl pan quickly.

6. Pour over steaks and serve.

This recipe is prepared most successfully when the skillet exactly holds the steaks.

sumptuous steak

1 boneless rib eye steak, broiled to
     desired state of doneness
1 onion, chopped
     cooking oil
1 large mushroom, sliced
3 chicken livers, finely chopped
½ C dry red wine
1 T slivered almonds

1. Saute the onion in the oil until translucent. Add the mushrooms and chopped
   chicken livers and cook through.

2. Add the wine, and simmer for 5 minutes
   more.

3. Place half of this sauce on a piece of
   aluminum foil large enough to securely
   enclose the steak.

4. Place the steak on top of the sauce. Add
   the remaining sauce over the steak.
   Sprinkle with almonds. Tightly seal the
   steak in foil.

5. Cook in a 500° oven for 4 minutes.

Serves 2.

This elegant dish is classically prepared in parchment paper. Foil serves equally well.

bifteck au poivre

4 boneless rib eye steaks, cut ½'' thick
3 T peppercorns
4 large mushroom caps
   cooking oil
4 toast rounds
5 T margarine
2 T dry red wine
2 T brandy
6 T liquid non-dairy creamer

1. Place peppercorns between 2 sheets of waxed paper. Roll with a rolling pin to crack.

2. Press cracked peppercorns into both sides of steaks and allow to stand at room temperature for 30 minutes.

3. Flute mushroom caps. Saute lightly in cooking oil. Set aside.

4. Arrange toast rounds on warm serving platter.

5. Heat the margarine in a frying pan.

6. Add steaks to pan and cook over high heat for about 5 minutes.

7. Turn the steaks with tongs and cook to desired state of doneness. Arrange on toast rounds.

8. Pour off excess grease from pan. Return pan to heat; deglaze with wine and brandy. Add non-dairy creamer and simmer.

9. Pour sauce over steaks. Garnish with mushroom caps and serve.

Ground pepper may not be substituted for cracked peppercorns.

steak dianne

2 boneless rib eye steaks, or prime
     shoulder steaks, cut ½'' thick
margarine
2 T shallots, chopped
1 T parsley, chopped
2 T margarine
1 T Worcestershire sauce
1 T steak sauce
2 T sherry
2 T brandy

1. Heat enough margarine to film the bottom of a frying pan.

2. Add steaks to pan and cook over high heat for about 4 minutes.

3. Turn the steaks with tongs and cook to desired state of doneness. Remove to a warm serving platter.

4. Combine shallots, parsley, 2 tablespoons margarine, Worcestershire sauce, steak sauce and sherry. Bring to a boil.

5. Remove from heat. Add brandy and flame while pouring over steaks.

A special dinner for two with candlelight and wine!

pepper steak

2 lbs. shoulder steak, sliced thin
2 cloves garlic, minced
2 T cooking oil
2 green Italian peppers, cut into strips
2 onions, sliced
6 oz. mushrooms, sliced
½ t pepper
½ t salt
¾ C dry red wine
¾ t curry powder

1. Saute 1 clove garlic in oil for 2 minutes. Add meat and brown. Remove meat from skillet. Discard garlic.

2. Saute peppers, onions and remaining garlic until tender. Add mushrooms, pepper, and salt and cook an additional 2 minutes. Add browned meat and wine. Cook slowly for 30 minutes.

3. Stir in curry powder and simmer 1 hour.

The meat should be sliced across the grain. Freeze slightly before cutting to facilitate a thin slice.

To eliminate knives when serving this recipe as a buffet dish, cut the meat into bite size pieces.

beef stroganoff

2 lbs. shoulder steak, sliced thin
6 T cooking oil
3½ T scallions, chopped
½ t tarragon
1 T Worcestershire sauce
1 T catsup
¼ t pepper
1½ C non-dairy sour cream

1. Brown meat quickly in cooking oil. Remove to a plate and keep warm.

2. Add scallions, tarragon, Worcestershire sauce, catsup and pepper to the pan and blend thoroughly over medium heat, cooking until the scallion is limp.

3. Turn the heat to warm and add the non-dairy sour cream, stirring constantly.

4. Spoon this sauce over the meat and serve immediately.

There are many versions of this tasty dish. Try this one and see if you don't agree that it's the best.

beef teriyaki

2 lbs. shoulder steak
1½ C soy sauce
¼ C sugar
1 clove garlic, minced
¼ C sherry
2 t ginger

1. Cut the steak into ⅛ inch slices.

2. Combine remaining ingredients. Bring to a boil; cool slightly.

3. Pour this marinade over the meat and marinate for at least 2 hours. Drain.

4. Thread the beef on small individual skewers.

5. Grill the beef over coals, or place under a broiler.

sukiyaki

1 lb. shoulder steak, sliced 1x4x⅛''
½ C soy sauce
1 C water
5 T sugar
½ C sherry
3 T cooking oil
8 oz. can bamboo shoots, cubed
6 scallions, cut into ½'' pieces
1 onion, cut into ½'' slices
6 mushrooms, sliced ¼'' thick
2 cakes bean curd, cut into 1'' cubes
2 oz. watercress or spinach

1. Combine soy sauce, water, sugar and sherry. Reserve.
2. Heat an electric skillet to 425°. Add oil and stir-fry meat.
3. Add vegetables and reserved sauce and cook 5 minutes. Serve immediately.

This recipe can be served over rice. Traditionally, shirataki noodles are added along with the vegetables.

For a dramatic presentation, prepare this dish at the table before your guests.

beef roulades

4 slices shoulder steak, cut ¼'' thick
   Dijon style mustard
   pepper
4 slices smoked dark meat turkey
2 sweet and sour pickles, sliced in half
4 T onion, chopped
2 T cooking oil
3 C beef broth

1. Spread each piece of meat with mustard. Sprinkle with pepper. Top with a slice of smoked turkey, a half pickle and 1 tablespoon of onion.
2. Roll up and tie securely.
3. Brown meat on all sides in very hot oil.
4. Add broth and cook over low heat for 2 hours or until tender. Turn from time to time and check liquid, adding more if needed.

Of course, one roulade serves one person — a great aid when planning a large party.

neat meat birds

8 slices shoulder steak,
  approx. 3½x6x¼''
¼ C horseradish
¼ C margarine, softened
8 slices smoked tongue, cut
  paper thin
 flour
3 T cooking oil
2 cloves garlic, minced
1 t thyme
1 C beef broth
4 T sherry

1. Pound the steaks between 2 pieces of waxed paper to flatten.

2. Combine the horseradish with the margarine. Spread this mixture on each slice of meat.

3. Place a slice of tongue over the mixture.

4. Roll and tie each meat bird. Flour lightly.

5. Brown the birds on all sides in cooking oil.

6. Add garlic, thyme and broth. Cover and simmer for 1 hour.

7. Add the sherry and cook an additional 30 minutes.

As good to taste as it is fun to pronounce.

sicilian braciole

6 slices shoulder steak,
   approx. 3½x6x¼''
6 slices smoked dark meat turkey
4 hard cooked eggs, sliced
3 cloves garlic, minced
9 T parsley, chopped
2 T olive oil
16 oz. can tomato sauce
1 t oregano
1 t basil
1 t capers
⅛ t pepper

1. Pound meat as thin as possible, between 2 pieces of waxed paper.

2. Top each slice of meat with a slice of smoked turkey and slices of hard cooked egg.

3. Combine garlic, and ½ cup of parsley and sprinkle over egg.

4. Roll each steak and tie securely with kitchen twine.

5. Brown meat on all sides in olive oil. Add tomato sauce, oregano, basil, capers, pepper and remaining parsley.

6. Simmer, covered, for 1½ hours.

Serve the Braciole with a side dish of spaghetti covered with the cooking sauce.

cold beef rolls

    4 slices shoulder steak,
        approx. 3½x6x½''
    ¼ t thyme
    1 clove garlic, minced
    3 T parsley, chopped
    1 onion, chopped
    ½ C vinegar
    1 bay leaf
    6 peppercorns
    ¼ t pepper
    1½ C bread crumbs
    4 T liquid non-dairy creamer
    6 scallions, minced
    1 pkg. frozen chopped spinach,
        thawed, squeezed
    3 hot kosher Italian sausages,
        remove casing, crumble
    1 egg, slightly beaten
    4 hard cooked eggs, chopped
    2 C beef broth

1. Pound steaks into a thin rectangle. Marinate for four hours in a marinade of thyme, garlic, 1 tablespoon parsley, onion, vinegar, bay leaf and peppercorns.

2. Drain and reserve marinade.

3. Sprinkle steaks with pepper.

4. Soak the bread crumbs in the non-dairy creamer. Add and mix in the scallions, spinach, the remaining parsley and the sausage. Add the beaten egg.

5. Spread this mixture over the meat. Sprinkle the chopped eggs over the spinach mixture. Roll and tie the meat securely.

6. Place in a roasting pan, pour marinade and beef broth over the meat; cover and cook in a 350° oven for 3 hours. Turn meat and baste often.

7. Cool. Cut into thin slices and serve cold.

This is a hearty meat meal, particularly effective as a summertime dish. It demands little to accompany it.

austrian pot roast

2 slices shoulder steak, cut
   ½'' thick
  pepper /
  flour
3 T cooking oil
3 onions, sliced
2 parsnips, sliced
2 carrots, sliced
3 T flour
½ t vinegar
2 C beef broth
1 T Worcestershire sauce

1. Pound meat to tenderize. Slash edges to prevent curling. Sprinkle steaks with pepper. Dredge in flour.

2. Brown steaks in cooking oil. Remove to a platter.

3. In the same oil, saute vegetables for 10 minutes.

4. Add flour, stirring until flour is absorbed.

5. Deglaze pan with vinegar and add broth. Return steak to the pan and simmer, covered, for 30 minutes.

6. Add Worcestershire sauce, stir and serve.

Pound meat with a metal or wooden meat tenderizing mallet.

london broil

1¾ lb. London Broil steak
2 T oil
1 T red wine vinegar
½ onion, chopped
1 t oregano
1 t garlic salt
½ t pepper
¼ t basil
¼ t rosemary

1. Combine all ingredients. Marinate steak in mixture for 6 hours. Turn frequently. Drain; reserve marinade.
2. Broil 3 inches from heat for 5 minutes.
3. Turn, brush with marinade and broil an additional 4 minutes.
4. To serve: slice diagonally across the grain.

For a change of pace, marinate the steak in **Oriental Marinade** *and either broil as directed, or cook over coals on an outdoor grill.*

oriental marinade

¼ C soy sauce
1 T oil
1 shallot, minced
1 clove garlic, minced
1 slice ginger root, minced
2 T sherry

Combine all ingredients well.

florentine steak

>   5 lb. London Broil, 2¼'' thick
>   ¼ C oil
>   ¼ C lemon juice
>   ½ t salt
>   ½ t pepper
>   lemon wedges
>   chopped parsley

1. Combine oil, lemon juice, salt and pepper.

2. Marinate meat for 30 minutes.

3. Broil 5 inches from heat for 20 minutes, brushing with marinade.

4. Turn steak and continue to broil and baste for an additional 20 minutes.

5. To serve: pour marinade over steak and slice thinly. Garnish with lemon wedges and parsley.

Note: Florentine in title refers to Florence, Italy. It does not indicate spinach.

Typically, Italian steak is always accompanied by a "bath". In this recipe the "bath" is used as a marinade and then as a dressing.

The simplicity of the recipe belies its tastiness.

swiss skillet steak

>   2½ lb. center cut chuck steak, bone-in
>   ¼ C flour
>   1 t salt
>   ¼ t pepper
>   2 T cooking oil
>   1 C onion, grated
>   1 carrot, grated
>   2 bay leaves
>   2 C water

1. Mix flour, salt and pepper. Rub both sides of steak with this mixture.

2. Brown meat on all sides in cooking oil. Remove meat to a plate.

3. In the same oil, saute onions and carrots for 10 minutes. Add bay leaves and water; return meat to pan.

4. Cover and simmer 2 hours or until meat is tender.

*Add **chopped tomatoes** along with the other vegetables, to make **Sicilian Skillet Steak.***

beef cutlets

4 minute steaks
¾ C bread crumbs
½ t garlic salt
¼ t pepper
1 T parsley, minced
1 egg mixed with 2 T water
   cooking oil

1. Mix bread crumbs with garlic salt, pepper and parsley.
2. Dip cutlets in egg mixture.
3. Press coated cutlets into bread crumb mixture.
4. Fry quickly in cooking oil on both sides. Drain and serve immediately.

Serrated steak may be substituted for minute steak.

Please note that these cutlets must be served immediately; they will become tough if allowed to stand.

Mushroom Sauce *may be served with these cutlets.*

mushroom sauce

½ lb. mushrooms, sliced
2 T margarine
2 T flour
1 C water
1 pkg. dry onion soup mix
2 T white wine
1 T soy sauce
2 T parsley, minced

1. Spread mushrooms on a greased cookie sheet and bake in a 400° oven for 30 minutes.
2. Melt margarine; stir in flour. Add water, onion soup mix, wine and soy sauce. Cook over medium heat, stirring until thick.
3. Remove from heat; stir in mushrooms and parsley.

chocolate pot roast

4 lb. boneless chuck roast
3 T cooking oil
1 clove garlic, minced
½ C onion, chopped
½ t salt
16 oz. can tomato sauce
½ C dry red wine
1 oz. unsweetened chocolate, melted
2 t sugar
1 tomato, cubed
1¼ t chili powder
1 t grated orange peel
¼ t cinnamon
½ t oregano
¼ t nutmeg
1 pkg. frozen carrots, thawed
1 jar onions, drained
⅓ C almonds, slivered

1. Brown meat in cooking oil. Pour off excess grease.

2. Add garlic, onion and salt. Stir until onion is translucent.

3. Combine tomato sauce, wine, chocolate, sugar, tomato and seasonings. Pour over meat.

4. Cover and simmer until meat is tender, about 3 hours.

5. Add vegetables and cook 10 additional minutes.

6. Remove to serving dish and sprinkle with nuts.

A typical dish south of the border. Chicken and other meats are very often prepared with chili and chocolate combinations.

sauerbraten

This recipe should be started one week in advance of serving. Plan ahead!

  4 lb. boneless chuck roast
  2 bay leaves
  1 clove garlic, crushed
  ½ C dark brown sugar
  ¾ C red wine vinegar
  ¾ C dry red wine
  2 C onions, sliced
  1 C carrots, sliced
  5 cloves
  ¼ t pepper
  ¾ C gingersnap crumbs

1. In a large container, place chuck roast with all ingredients, except gingersnap crumbs. Add cold water to cover meat. Place a tight lid over container and refrigerate for seven days, turning the meat occasionally.

2. Remove meat from marinade and pat dry. Reserve marinade.

3. Brown meat on all sides in cooking oil. Add marinade, cover and simmer 2 hours. Remove meat to a carving board.

4. Strain the marinade into a small pot. Bring to a boil. Slowly add the gingersnap crumbs, stirring constantly, until thickened.

5. Slice meat thinly, and arrange on serving platter. Spoon the thickened sauce over the sliced meat and serve.

This recipe is so tasty, it is well worth the inconvenience of having a large container in the refrigerator for a week.

italian pot roast

3 lb. boneless chuck roast
2 T cooking oil
¼ C green peppers, chopped
½ C onions, chopped
15 oz. can tomatoes
6 oz. can tomato paste
1½ T Worcestershire sauce
2 bay leaves
1 t basil
¼ t salt
¼ t pepper

1. Brown meat in cooking oil. Remove to a plate.
2. Saute peppers and onions until limp.
3. Return to the pan and add tomatoes and remaining ingredients.
4. Simmer, covered, for 2½ hours.

The long, slow process of braising, or pot roasting, causes the fibers to break down, making the meat tender.

potted pot roast

3 lb. boneless chuck roast
2 T flour
¼ t garlic salt
¼ t paprika
⅛ t pepper
2 T cooking oil
½ C beef broth
¼ C Scotch whiskey

1. Combine flour with salt, paprika and pepper. Dredge beef in this mixture.
2. Brown meat on all sides in cooking oil.
3. Add beef broth and Scotch.
4. Reduce heat to low, cover and cook 2 hours.

Suggested pot roasts are: shoulder, boneless chuck, brisket, and top of the rib.

swedish pot roast

5 lb. boneless chuck roast
4 T cooking oil
1 C onions, chopped
2 cloves garlic, minced
⅓ C flour
¼ C red wine vinegar
1 t salt
2 T dark corn syrup
2 C beef broth
2 bay leaves
4 sprigs parsley
1 t whole peppercorns

1. Brown the roast in cooking oil. Remove to a plate.

2. Saute onions and garlic until limp. Stir in flour. Add vinegar, salt, corn syrup and broth. Stir to mix well.

3. Return roast to pan and add bay leaves, parsley and peppercorns. Cover and simmer 3 hours.

4. Place roast on a serving platter. Strain some sauce over the roast and pass remaining sauce in gravy boat.

The flavor of a pot roast is always enhanced by reheating. Cook at your own convenience.

saucey brisket

3 lb. brisket
3 T oil
2 onions, grated
2 carrots, grated
2 T parsley, minced
½ t garlic powder
1 C beef broth
2 T apricot preserves

1. Sear meat in cooking oil on both sides.

2. Mix remaining ingredients together and add to the meat.

3. Add enough water to ensure at least ½ inch of liquid in the pot at all times.

4. Cover and simmer about 3 hours or until meat is tender.

5. Remove meat, slice and return to pot. Cook an additional 10 minutes.

Quartered potatoes may be added 30 minutes before the meat is finished cooking.

For those watching calories: omit the apricot preserves and add two stalks of celery and a tomato in their stead.

pot au feu

4 lb. brisket
6 qt. water
½ t salt
½ small cabbage, cut into wedges
3 leeks, cut into 2'' pieces
2 carrots, cut into 2'' pieces
1 onion stuck with 3 cloves
1 parsnip, cut into 2'' pieces
1 turnip, cut into 2'' pieces
   bouquet garni:
   2 sprigs parsley
   ¼ t thyme
   1 bay leaf
   1 t peppercorns

Combine all ingredients and cook for 3 hours, skimming when necessary.

There are several ways to serve this classic French boiled beef dinner.

One may strain the broth and serve it as a soup course with croutons or with a crusty French bread. Follow this with the meat arranged in the center of a platter surrounded by vegetable bouquets.

One may also serve a meal in a dish. Place a toast round in an individual soup bowl, and then add the broth, the meat cut into chunks and a complete selection of the vegetables.

*To serve as **Petite Marmite**, place a selection of meat and vegetables and some beef broth in individual casseroles. Cover with a thin slice of toast which has been spread with a paste made of **4 ounces of tofu, 2 egg yolks, ¼ t garlic salt, 1 T oil**. Bake in a 375° oven until golden.*

salade parisienne

4 lb. brisket, boiled, drained, chilled
   overnight
  romaine lettuce
6 hard cooked eggs, sliced
1 large onion, sliced, separated
   into rings
4 potatoes, boiled, sliced, chilled
3 tomatoes, quartered
½ C green beans, cooked, chilled
½ C julienne carrots, cooked, chilled
2 T capers
1 recipe Parisienne Dressing
2 T parsley, chopped
1 T chives, minced

1. Cut the cold meat into large cubes.
2. Arrange a bed of romaine on a serving platter. Layer on the beef, eggs, vegetables and capers. Drizzle the dressing over. Garnish with parsley and chives.

This salad makes a good summer picnic.

parisienne dressing

10 T olive oil
 4 T red wine vinegar
 1 t garlic salt
 1 t pepper
 2 t Dijon style mustard

Combine all ingredients well.

glazed corned beef I

1 corned beef, cooked
2 T chicken fat
1 T prepared mustard
5 T catsup
3 T cider vinegar
1 C brown sugar

1. Bring all ingredients except meat to a boil and stir well.

2. Pour sauce over corned beef and roast in a 350° oven for 30 minutes. Baste often.

This dish can be served hot, directly from the oven, or it can be sliced and served at room temperature.

Braised Cabbage *complements it nicely, as does cold* **Carrot Salad**.

glazed corned beef II

1 corned beef, cooked
   cloves
½ C orange juice
½ t ground cloves
1 t prepared mustard
½ C brown sugar
   pineapple rings
   cherries

1. Score corned beef lightly with a knife, creating a diamond pattern.

2. In the center of each diamond, stud one clove. Place meat into roasting pan.

3. Mix together the orange juice, ground cloves, mustard and sugar. Pour over beef.

4. Place pineapple rings decoratively on top of beef. Place a cherry in the center of each pineapple.

5. Bake in a 350° oven for 30 minutes, basting frequently.

Serve with **Mustard Cream**.

mustard cream

2 T margarine
2 T flour
2 T dry mustard
1 T sugar
1 t salt
  dash cayenne pepper
1 C liquid non-dairy creamer
1 egg, beaten
2 T cider vinegar

1. Melt margarine; stir in flour, mustard, sugar, salt and cayenne. Cook, stirring constantly until just bubbly.

2. Stir in liquid non-dairy creamer and continue cooking and stirring until sauce thickens and boils, about 1 minute.

3. Stir ½ cup hot mixture into beaten egg. Then add tempered egg to remaining sauce in pan. Cook, stirring constantly, 1 minute longer. Remove from heat and stir in vinegar. Chill.

4. Before serving beat until smooth.

corned beef hash

1 lb. cooked corned beef, chilled
3 small potatoes, cooked, chilled
1 onion
1 t prepared mustard
¼ t pepper
¼ t nutmeg
5 T margarine
2 poached eggs

1. Grind the corned beef and onion together.

2. Coarsely chop the potatoes and add to the meat mixture.

3. Add the seasonings.

4. Melt the margarine in a heavy skillet. Add the hash mixture and pack down. Cook until a crust is formed. Turn and cook on the other side until crusty.

5. Remove to plate, top with eggs and serve.

Try this dish for breakfast or for your next brunch.

old fashioned corned beef

5 lb. corned beef
3 onions studded with 3 cloves
6 peppercorns
1 bay leaf
½ t rosemary
1 clove garlic
2 green pepper rings
1 stalk celery
1 carrot
3 sprigs parsley
1 t wine vinegar

1. In a very large sauce pot, cover corned beef with cold water and bring to a boil. Remove corned beef and drain.

2. Again place corned beef in pot, cover with cold water, bring to a boil and add remaining ingredients.

3. Simmer 4 to 5 hours or until tender.

Serve with **Raisin Sauce.**

To make this into a complete **New England Boiled Dinner** *add* **carrots, potatoes** *and* **cabbage** *and boil an additional 30 minutes.*

raisin sauce

½ C brown sugar
1½ t dry mustard
1 T cornstarch
1½ C water
¼ C vinegar
⅓ C raisins

1. Combine sugar, mustard and cornstarch.

2. Slowly add water and vinegar. Add raisins.

3. Cook, covered, over low heat for 10 minutes, stirring constantly until thick and bubbly.

sicilian boiled beef

2 lbs. flanken
water to cover
1 carrot, sliced
1 onion, sliced
1 stalk celery, sliced
1 leek, sliced
1 parsnip, halved
½ t salt
5 peppercorns
1 recipe Italian Tomato Sauce I
1 recipe Roasted Italian Peppers
noodles, cooked
Italian bread

1. Combine meat, water, raw vegetables, salt and pepper. Bring to a boil, reduce heat and simmer 2 hours. Skim as often as necessary.

2. Remove meat; reserve cooking liquid. Cut the meat into bite size pieces.

3. Combine meat, tomato sauce and peppers. Heat all together.

4. Strain cooking liquid. Reheat with cooked noodles and serve as a soup course.

5. Then serve the meat with warm Italian bread.

barbequed beef ribs and three sauces

1. Select 3 pounds well trimmed short ribs of beef.

2. Bring desired sauce to a boil.

3. Pour sauce over ribs, cover and bake in a 350° oven for 1 hour; then uncover and bake for an additional 30 minutes in a 375° oven, or until nicely browned. After the hour, ribs may be removed to a rack and placed under the broiler to brown.

I

½ C vinegar
1 T hot sauce
1 t Worcestershire sauce
½ C catsup
1 T oil
¼ t salt
3 T brown sugar
½ t garlic powder
1 onion, sliced
3 T parsley, chopped
1 T basil
½ t pepper
1 t dry mustard
½ t oregano

II

1 C tomato sauce
1 C water
¼ C vinegar
1 T sugar
1 T prepared mustard
1 t salt
¼ t pepper
2 onions, minced
2 T parsley, minced

III

2 scallions, chopped
2 cloves garlic, crushed
1 T chili sauce
2 T catsup
3 T soy sauce
3 T brown sugar
½ C honey
½ C pineapple juice
2 t lemon juice
½ t dry mustard
1 t prepared mustard
¼ t powdered ginger

puchero de carne

2½ lbs. short ribs
2 qt. water
1 t salt
1 t pepper
2 onions, halved
3 carrots, cut into 3″ pieces
½ lb. cabbage, cut into wedges
3 sweet kosher Italian sausages
3 cloves garlic, minced
2 potatoes, halved
1 yellow squash, cut into chunks
1 Italian pepper, cut into strips
1 pkg. frozen corn, thawed, drained
2 tomatoes, quartered
1 lb. 4 oz. can chick peas, drained

1. Place beef, water, salt and pepper in a large pot. Bring to a boil and skim surface. Simmer, covered, for 1½ hours.

2. Add onions, carrots, cabbage, sausages, garlic and potatoes. Bring to a boil and simmer 3 minutes.

3. Add squash and green pepper. Cook an additional 10 minutes.

4. Add corn, tomatoes and chick peas. Simmer 5 minutes.

5. Pour off broth and reserve.

6. Cut meat into serving pieces and arrange with vegetables on a serving plate.

It is customary to skim the fat from the broth and serve the broth over a toast round, as a first course.

braised short ribs of beef

2½ lbs. short ribs
3 T cooking oil
1 C onions, sliced
½ t salt
½ t garlic powder
½ t pepper
1 carrot, cut into 1″ pieces
2 stalks celery, cut into 1″ pieces
1 tomato, chopped
1 C beef broth
1 T Worcestershire sauce

1. Brown meat in cooking oil.
2. Add remaining ingredients and simmer, covered, for 3 hours, or until meat is tender.

Short ribs of beef are one of the most flavorable cuts of meat for braising; however, the yield is meager. Any meal planned around a short ribs entree should contain hearty side dishes.

boeuf bourguignonne

4 lbs. boneless beef for stewing, cut into cubes

4 onions, chopped

3 C dry red wine

1 bay leaf

3 sprigs parsley

½ t thyme

2 T olive oil

¼ t salt

¼ t pepper

1 clove garlic, crushed

cooking oil

2 T flour

¼ C brandy

½ C water

2 leeks, sliced

2 carrots, sliced

4 slices beef fry, cooked, chopped

24 small white onions, boiled, drained

2 T sugar

3 T margarine

1 t lemon juice

8 oz. mushroom caps

2 T parsley, chopped

1. Combine onions, wine, bay leaf, parsley, thyme, olive oil, salt, pepper and garlic to make a marinade.

2. Marinate the beef for 4 hours in the prepared marinade. Remove meat, strain marinade and reserve.

3. Pat meat dry and brown in cooking oil. Add flour and cook 2 minutes, stirring constantly. Add brandy and bring to a boil.

4. Add reserved marinade and water and bring to a boil.

5. Add leeks, carrots and beef fry, and bring to a boil. Cover, reduce heat and simmer 2 hours.

6. Melt margarine and sugar together. Add the onions and cook until lightly browned. Remove to a warm plate. Add the mushrooms to the same pan, sprinkle with lemon juice and then brown the mushrooms.

7. To serve: pour meat with its gravy into a deep serving dish. Add onions and arrange mushrooms on top. Sprinkle with parsley.

This dish may also be cooked in a 350° oven for 2 hours.

beef carbonnade

3 lbs. boneless beef for stewing,
    cut into cubes
¼ t salt
½ t pepper
4 T flour
4 T cooking oil
6 onions, sliced
2 cloves garlic, crushed
1½ C beef broth
1½ C beer
    bouquet garni:
        3 sprigs parsley
        1 celery top
        1 bay leaf
        1 t thyme
        4 peppercorns
1 T brown sugar
1 T vinegar

1. Mix flour, salt and pepper. Dredge meat in this mixture.

2. Brown meat in cooking oil; remove to a plate.

3. Add onions and garlic and cook until limp.

4. Add beef broth, beer and the bouquet garni.

5. Return meat to pan and bring to a boil. Reduce heat, cover and simmer 3 hours.

6. Remove bouquet garni; add sugar and vinegar and simmer an additional 10 minutes.

Excellent with noodles or parsley potatoes. Beer may be served with this meal.

brown stew

2 lbs. boneless beef for stewing, cut into cubes

2 T cooking oil

4 C boiling water

1 t lemon juice

1 t Worcestershire sauce

1 clove garlic

1 onion, sliced

2 bay leaves

1 t salt

½ t pepper

½ t paprika

½ t allspice

1 t sugar

1. Brown meat in cooking oil, slowly, carefully and thoroughly on all sides.

2. Add remaining ingredients and simmer 2 hours.

Peeled carrots, cut into 2 inch pieces and small whole white onions may be added during the last half hour. Do be sure to serve something with color on the same plate to please the eye as well as the palate.

easy stew

1 lb. boneless beef for stewing, cut into cubes

¼ C bread crumbs

¼ C flour

⅛ t pepper

½ C dry red wine

2 beef bouillon cubes dissolved in 1¼ C water

1. Do not brown meat. Combine all ingredients in a casserole.

2. Cover and bake in a 300° oven for 3 hours.

Of course, the joy of this recipe is in preparing it; the delight is in tasting it.

hungarian beef goulash

3 lbs. boneless beef for stewing,
     cut into cubes
4 T cooking oil
3 onions, chopped
6 T Hungarian paprika
6 tomatoes, chopped
¼ C beef broth

1. Brown meat in cooking oil. Set aside.

2. Saute onions in cooking oil until limp.

3. Stir in paprika and cook 2 minutes.

4. Return meat to pan. Add tomatoes and beef broth and simmer, covered, for 3 hours. Occasionally shake the pan to prevent burning. Do not remove the cover during the cooking process.

Do not add pepper to this dish; it will spoil the taste of the paprika.

beef and bow casserole

1 lb. lean ground beef
2 T cooking oil
¼ C onion, chopped
1 lb. 12 oz. can tomatoes,
    reserve ¼ C liquid
½ C dark corn syrup
¼ t pepper
½ t chili powder
1 bay leaf
2 T cornstarch
3 C cooked bows, drained
  bread crumbs

1. Saute onion in cooking oil until limp.

2. Add beef and brown thoroughly.

3. Add tomatoes, corn syrup and seasonings. Bring to a boil. Cover and simmer 15 minutes.

4. Mix cornstarch with reserved tomato liquid. Add to pan and bring to a boil, stirring constantly until thickened.

5. Add bows. Mix well and turn into a 2 quart casserole. Sprinkle top with bread crumbs.

6. Bake in a 350° oven for 30 minutes.

This casserole travels well, making it a good dish for P.T.A. meetings or other occasions when a covered dish is requested.

moussaka

1 lb. lean ground beef
2 onions, chopped
2 T cooking oil
½ t salt
¼ t pepper
dash of cinnamon
¼ C red wine
8 oz. can tomato sauce
1 T tomato paste
¼ C parsley, chopped
1 egg, beaten
½ C bread crumbs
2 large eggplants
1 recipe Moussaka Sauce

1. Saute onion in cooking oil until limp. Add the meat and seasonings and brown thoroughly. Add wine, tomato sauce, tomato paste and parsley and cook until all liquid is absorbed.

2. Add egg and ¼ cup bread crumbs and set aside.

3. Cut eggplant into ½ inch slices. Brush both sides with oil and broil on both sides until soft.

4. Grease casserole and sprinkle with ¼ cup bread crumbs.

5. Put one layer of eggplant in casserole, add meat sauce and continue to layer eggplant and sauce. Top with **Moussaka Sauce**. Cover sauce with more bread crumbs and bake in a 350° oven for 45 minutes.

moussaka sauce

3 T margarine
3 T flour
2 egg yolks, slightly beaten
1½ C liquid non-dairy creamer
⅛ t pepper
½ t nutmeg

Melt margarine; stir in flour and cook for 2 minutes, stirring constantly. Gradually add the non-dairy creamer and egg yolks and cook until thick. Add pepper and nutmeg.

Beef or lamb, or a combination of both may be used in this classic Greek dish.

chili con carne

1 lb. ground beef
2 T cooking oil
1 t salt
3 T chili powder
⅓ C onions, chopped
8 oz. can tomato sauce
15 oz. can red kidney beans, drained
2 T vinegar
⅛ t garlic powder

1. Brown beef in cooking oil.
2. Add remaining ingredients, cover and simmer 45 minutes.

A great favorite of the West has come to the East.

sweet and sour meat loaf

    1 lb. ground beef
    1 onion, minced
   12 snack crackers, crushed
   ¼ t black pepper
   ¼ t salt
    8 oz. can tomato sauce
    1 egg, beaten
    2 T vinegar
   ¼ t dry mustard
    2 T brown sugar
   ⅔ C water

1. In a 9 inch pie plate, mix together the beef, onion, crackers, pepper, salt, ½ cup tomato sauce and the egg. Form into a round mound one inch smaller than the pie plate.

2. Mix together remaining tomato sauce, vinegar, mustard, and brown sugar. Pour over meat loaf. Pour water around edge of loaf.

3. Bake in a 350° oven for one hour.

4. Cut into slices and serve with sauce from plate.

This is one of the best meat loaves ever. It's especially nice because it has its own sauce; and it's a real quickie to prepare.

sweet and sour meatballs

1½ lbs. ground beef
4 T onion, grated
1 egg
1 t salt
⅛ t pepper
3 T cornstarch
2 T cooking oil
2 beef bouillon cubes dissolved in ½ C water
2 T lemon juice
1 lemon, thinly sliced
¼ C dark raisins
3 T sugar
6 gingersnaps, crushed

1. Mix together the meat, onion, egg, salt and pepper. Shape into one inch balls. Roll the balls in cornstarch.

2. Brown meatballs in cooking oil.

3. Add broth, lemon juice, lemon slices, raisins and sugar.

4. Cover and cook over low heat for 35 minutes.

5. Stir in gingersnaps and cook an additional 10 minutes.

italian meatballs

1 lb. ground beef
¼ C bread crumbs
2 eggs, slightly beaten
3 T onion, minced
2 T dry red wine
4 T parsley, minced
2 T basil, minced
1 t garlic salt
½ t pepper
   cooking oil

1. Add bread crumbs to eggs. Allow to stand for 5 minutes.

2. Combine beef, egg mixture, onion, wine, parsley, basil, salt and pepper, mixing together quickly and gently with fingertips. Do not over-handle.

3. Form into 2 inch balls.

4. Fry slowly in cooking oil until well browned and cooked through.

Combine this dish with **Italian Tomato Sauce I** *and* **Roasted Italian Peppers**.

lasagne

1 lb. ground beef
1 lb. sweet kosher Italian sausage, casing removed, crumbled
1 onion, chopped
16 oz. can tomato sauce
3 oz. tomato paste
½ t salt
½ t pepper
½ t oregano
1 T basil
12 oz. tofu
4 egg yolks
4 t oil
1½ t garlic salt
1 T parsley
6 lasagne noodles, boiled, drained

1. Brown the meat, sausage and onion in a skillet.

2. Add tomato sauce, tomato paste, salt, pepper, oregano, and basil. Simmer, uncovered for 30 minutes.

3. Combine the tofu, egg yolks, oil, garlic salt and parsley and puree in a blender or a food processor. Reserve ¼ cup of this mixture for topping.

4. To assemble: grease a 1½ quart rectangular baking dish. Layer 3 noodles, spread half of the tofu mixture over the noodles; cover with half of the meat sauce; repeat, ending with meat sauce. Noodles should be completely covered. Place dollops of reserved tofu mixture over top. Spread out slightly.

5. Bake in a 375° oven for 25 minutes until bubbling.

Now stand back and be prepared for comments. This dish looks and tastes like the McCoy.

italian tomato sauce II

1 lb. ground beef
¼ C bread crumbs
2 eggs, slightly beaten
3 T onion, minced
2 T dry red wine
8 T parsley, minced
6 T basil, minced
2 t garlic salt
1 t pepper
35 oz. can whole tomatoes
8 oz. can tomato sauce
1 onion, chopped
½ t oregano
1 t capers, packed in salt, rinsed
1 t sugar
¼ lb. flanken
¼ lb. kosher Italian sausage

1. Add bread crumbs to eggs. Allow to stand for 5 minutes.

2. Combine beef, egg mixture, minced onion, wine, 4 tablespoons parsley, 2 tablespoons basil, 1 teaspoon garlic salt and ½ teaspoon pepper; mix together quickly and gently with fingertips. Do not over-handle.

3. Form into 2 inch balls.

4. Combine all the remaining ingredients, except meat. Crush tomatoes. Bring to a boil.

5. Add flanken and sausage. Drop in meatballs.

6. Cook, covered, for 45 minutes.

Serve this sauce over pasta at a family-style dinner.

veal cordon blue

12 veal scallops, pounded thin
    (shoulder sliced thin)

    hoummous

 6 slices smoked dark meat turkey,
    sliced very thin

 6 slices tofu, cut very thin

    flour

 1 egg mixed with 1 T water

    bread crumbs

    cooking oil

1. Layer as follows to make a sandwich:
    1 slice veal, spread with a thin coating of hoummous
    1 slice smoked dark meat turkey
    1 slice tofu spread with a thin coating of hoummous
    1 slice veal

2. Dip sandwich in flour, egg mixture and then bread crumbs.

3. Fry in oil, on both sides, until golden brown.

Here you see the classic Cordon Bleu — minus cheese — with a new twist. We think you'll enjoy this new combination of textures and flavors.

florentine saltimbocca

2 lbs. veal scallops
  (shoulder sliced thin)
  flour, mixed with salt and pepper
6 T cooking oil
½ t sage
1 T parsley, minced
  smoked dark meat turkey, sliced
  thin
½ C margarine
⅔ C sweet sherry
2 pkgs. frozen spinach, thawed,
  squeezed
2 hard cooked eggs, sliced into
  rounds

1. Pound the scallops very thin between 2 pieces of waxed paper. Flour lightly.

2. Saute the veal slowly in the cooking oil, about 6 minutes on each side, until golden brown. Remove to a warm platter.

3. Sprinkle each scallop with sage and parsley. Top with a slice of smoked turkey.

4. Melt ¼ cup margarine, add veal topped with turkey. Add the sherry to the pan and simmer 10 minutes.

5. Heat spinach in ¼ cup margarine. Remove to a serving platter.

6. Place the veal on top of the spinach and top each veal scallop with a slice of egg. Pour pan juices over all.

Although "saltimbocca" means "jump in the mouth", this interesting vegetable and meat combination is not a hot spicy dish.

Lettuce may be substituted for the spinach, according to taste.

escalopes de veau saute chasseur
veal scallops hunter style

2 lbs. veal scallops
  (shoulder sliced thin)
  flour, mixed with salt and pepper
3 T margarine
10 mushrooms, sliced
3 shallots, minced
¼ C dry white wine
8 oz. can tomato sauce
1 T parsley, chopped
½ t tarragon

1. Pound the scallops very thin between 2 pieces of waxed paper. Flour lightly.

2. Saute the veal slowly in the margarine, about 6 minutes on each side, until golden brown. Remove to a warm plate.

3. Add the mushrooms and shallots to the pan and cook until soft.

4. Add the wine and cook vigorously for 5 minutes.

5. Add the tomato sauce and cook until reduced by half.

6. Add the parsley and tarragon.

7. Pour the sauce over the meat and serve.

It is appropriate to garnish any dish prepared "au chasseur" with minced mushrooms.

escalopes de veau
veal scallops

2 lbs. veal scallops,
   (shoulder sliced thin)
flour, mixed with salt and pepper
4 T margarine
⅔ C dry white wine
1 t chopped chives
1 t tarragon
1 t parsley, chopped
2 T margarine, softened

1. Pound the scallops very thin between 2 pieces of waxed paper. Flour lightly.

2. Saute the veal slowly in the margarine, about 6 minutes on each side, until golden brown. Remove to a warm platter.

3. Add wine to pan drippings. Reduce to half over high heat.

4. Add herbs, swirl in softened margarine until just melted. Pour over meat and serve.

vitello al carciofini
veal with artichokes

2 lbs. veal scallops
   (shoulder sliced thin)
flour, mixed with salt and pepper
cooking oil
1 lb. can tomatoes
½ t garlic salt
½ C sherry
¼ t oregano
2 pkgs. frozen artichoke hearts,
   thawed, drained

1. Pound the scallops very thin between 2 pieces of waxed paper. Flour lightly.

2. Saute the veal slowly in the cooking oil, about 6 minutes on each side, until golden brown.

3. Add tomatoes, garlic salt, wine and oregano. Gently mix in artichoke hearts.

4. Cover and simmer 30 minutes.

lemon veal

2 lbs. veal scallops
(shoulder sliced thin)
flour, mixed with salt and pepper
6 T margarine
½ t salt
½ C dry white wine
3 T lemon juice
6 sprigs parsley

1. Pound the scallops very thin between 2 pieces of waxed paper. Flour lightly.

2. Saute the veal slowly in the margarine, about 6 minutes on each side, until golden brown. Sprinkle with salt.

3. To skillet, add wine and lemon juice; bring to a boil.

4. Serve immediately with sprigs of fresh parsley.

wienerschnitzel

2 lbs. veal cutlets, pounded very thin
(boneless shoulder)
flour, mixed with salt and pepper
2 eggs mixed with 2 T water
bread crumbs
cooking oil
lemon slices
parsley, chopped
capers, minced
stuffed olives, sliced

1. Dredge veal lightly in flour.

2. Dip veal into beaten egg mixture.

3. Then dip into bread crumbs.

4. Fry in cooking oil on both sides until golden and cooked through.

5. Garnish each cutlet with a slice of lemon sprinkled with parsley and capers. Place an olive slice in the center of the lemon slice. Serve Immediately.

Do not allow the veal to rest after it is breaded. It should be fried immediately.

To serve as **Wienerschnitzel Holstein,** *garnish with a* **fried egg.**

veal cutlets tofunetti

2 lbs. veal cutlets, pounded thin
(boneless shoulder)
2 eggs mixed with 2 T water
1 C bread crumbs
4 T cooking oil
1 recipe Tomato Sauce I
8 oz. tofu
3 egg yolks
2 t garlic salt

1. Dip cutlets in egg mixture and then in bread crumbs.
2. Fry quickly in cooking oil until brown on both sides.
3. Remove to a baking dish. Top with tomato sauce.
4. Blend together tofu, egg yolks and garlic salt.
5. Spread tofu mixture over each cutlet.
6. Bake in a 350° oven for 30 minutes.

This recipe is Veal Parmesean masquerading under a new name.

veal francais

2 lbs. veal cutlets, pounded thin
(boneless shoulder)
2 eggs mixed with 2 T water
bread crumbs
cooking oil
1 C chicken broth
1 T lemon juice
lemon slices
parsley, chopped

1. Dip cutlets in egg mixture and then in bread crumbs.
2. Fry quickly in oil until golden brown on both sides.
3. Add chicken broth and lemon juice. Cover and simmer 15 minutes.
4. Garnish with lemon slices and parsley.

cotolette al vino

2 lbs. veal cutlets, pounded thin
  (boneless shoulder)
2 eggs mixed with 2 T water
  bread crumbs
4 T cooking oil
¼ lb. mushrooms, sliced thin
¾ C beef broth
½ C sweet white wine
1 hard cooked egg, minced
2 T parsley, chopped
1 T capers

1. Dip cutlets in egg mixture and then in bread crumbs.

2. Fry quickly in oil until golden brown on both sides. Remove to plate.

3. Add mushrooms to skillet and stir to coat with pan drippings. Add broth and wine. Return veal to pan. Cover and simmer 15 minutes.

4. Combine parsley, capers and egg.

5. To serve: arrange veal on warm platter. Pour mushrooms and pan juices over meat. Sprinkle with chopped egg mixed with parsley and capers.

Traditionally made with Marsala wine, this dish now takes on a new title.

paupiettes de veau

1½ lbs. shoulder of veal, cut thin,
         pounded
 ½ lb. mushrooms, minced
 1 T margarine
 1 T flour
 ½ C liquid non-dairy creamer
 ¼ t salt
 ¼ t white pepper
         flour
 3 T margarine
 ¼ C dry vermouth
 ½ C sherry
 ½ C chicken broth

1. Saute mushrooms in 1 tablespoon margarine until mushrooms are soft.

2. Add flour and stir well. Add non-dairy creamer, salt and pepper. Continue to cook until thick. Set aside.

3. Spread some of the mushroom mixture on each veal slice. Roll and tie securely.

4. Sprinkle with flour and saute in margarine until brown. Place in a baking dish.

5. Combine vermouth, sherry and chicken broth, bring to a boil and reduce to one half. Pour sauce over veal.

6. Bake in a 350° oven for 20 minutes.

veal rollitini

1½ lbs. shoulder of veal, cut thin,
     pounded
 1 onion, minced
 7 T margarine
 ½ C parsley, minced
 1 C bread crumbs
 ¼ t salt
 ¼ t white pepper
 ½ t thyme
 ½ t marjoram
 ½ t basil
    flour
1½ C beef broth
 1 bay leaf

1. Saute onion in 3 tablespoons margarine until translucent.

2. Stir in parsley, bread crumbs and seasonings.

3. Spread some of the bread crumb mixture on each piece of veal. Roll up and tie securely.

4. Sprinkle with flour. Saute veal birds in remaining margarine until lightly browned. Then add beef broth and bay leaf and simmer, covered, for about 40 minutes.

5. Remove bay leaf before serving.

savory veal rolls

1½ lbs. shoulder of veal, sliced thin, pounded
¾ C smoked dark meat turkey, chopped
1 clove garlic, minced
3 shallots, minced
3 T parsley, chopped
¼ t salt
⅛ t white pepper
flour
4 T cooking oil
1 C dry white wine
2 C chicken stock
1 carrot, chopped
1 onion, chopped
1 stalk celery, chopped
½ t rosemary

1. Combine turkey, garlic, shallots, 2 tablespoons parsley, salt and pepper.

2. Spread some of this mixture on each veal slice; roll and tie securely.

3. Sprinkle with flour. Brown in cooking oil.

4. Add wine and cook over medium heat 10 minutes.

5. Add remaining ingredients, cover and simmer 20 minutes.

Serve this dish with **Polenta;** *it will be enhanced by the rich gravy.*

veal birds

1½ lbs. shoulder of veal, sliced thin, pounded
2 T parsley, chopped
2 scallions, minced
½ t salt
¼ t pepper
4 strips beef fry, minced
1 T imitation-bacon flavored bits
1 T onion, chopped
2 T celery, chopped
2 T cooking oil
¼ C chicken broth

1. Combine parsley, scallions, salt, pepper, beef fry, imitation-bacon flavored bits, onion, and celery.

2. Saute this mixture in cooking oil. Cool.

3. Spread some of this mixture on each veal slice. Roll and tie securely.

4. Brown the birds in cooking oil. Add chicken broth, cover and simmer 1 hour.

Use either ready made imitation-bacon flavored bits; or fry a look alike vegetarian breakfast strip and crumble it.

veal cacciatora

2 lbs. boneless veal shoulder, sliced thin
6 T cooking oil
¼ t salt
¼ t white pepper
¼ lb. mushrooms, sliced
½ C onion, minced
2 green peppers, sliced
1 clove garlic, minced
1 C canned tomatoes, chopped
½ C dry white wine
½ t oregano
¼ t sugar
1 bay leaf

1. Pound veal slices very thin between 2 pieces of waxed paper.

2. Sprinkle with salt and pepper.

3. Saute veal lightly in cooking oil. Remove to a plate.

4. Add mushrooms, onion, green peppers, garlic and saute until vegetables are tender.

5. Add the sauteed veal, tomatoes, wine, oregano, sugar and bay leaf. Simmer for 20 minutes.

veal roulades

8 slices serrated shoulder of veal,
    pounded thin
½ C onion, sliced
5 T margarine
1 C bread crumbs
1 t tarragon
1 t basil
1 T parsley, chopped
8 slices smoked dark meat turkey
2 T brandy
1 bay leaf
½ C dry white wine
1 C chicken broth
3 T flour mixed with ¼ C water

1. Saute onion in 2 tablespoons margarine. Remove from heat and add bread crumbs, tarragon, basil and parsley; toss to combine.

2. Place 2 tablespoons of crumb mixture on each piece of veal; top with a slice of turkey. Roll and tie securely.

3. In remaining margarine, brown veal on all sides. Remove from heat.

4. Warm brandy; ignite and pour over the veal rolls. Add bay leaf, wine and chicken broth.

5. Bring to a boil and simmer, covered, 30 to 40 minutes. Remove veal to heated platter.

6. Measure pan liquid and add water, if necessary, to make 1¾ cups. Return liquid to skillet.

7. Stir flour mixture into skillet. Bring to a boil and stir until thick. Pour over veal and serve.

veal birds tofunetti

6 slices serrated shoulder of veal,
    pounded thin
4 oz. tofu
2 t garlic salt
1 egg yolk
6 slices smoked dark meat turkey
6 scallions, cut 3″ long
    cooking oil
9 mushrooms, sliced
1 C dry white wine
¼ t salt
¼ t white pepper

1. Blend the tofu, garlic salt and egg yolk into a smooth paste.

2. Place a piece of turkey and some of the tofu mixture on each slice of veal.

3. Roll the veal up, enclosing a scallion in each bird. Tie securely with string.

4. Brown the birds in cooking oil. Remove from pan.

5. Add mushrooms to pan and brown. Deglaze with wine; add salt and pepper.

6. Return birds to pan and cook gently about 10 minutes, until done. Serve with sauce.

The scallion in this dish provides an unexpected taste treat.

veal with rice

1½ lbs. serrated veal shoulder steaks
1 onion, sliced thin
   cooking oil
¼ lb. sweet kosher Italian sausage,
   cut into 3″ pieces
2 C rice, uncooked
1 C canned tomatoes, chopped
2 T parsley, chopped
4 C chicken broth
¼ C water
¼ t salt
½ t white pepper

1. Saute onion in 2 tablespoons cooking oil until translucent. Add sausage and cook 5 minutes. Stir in rice, tomatoes and parsley; cook 5 minutes.

2. Add chicken broth, cover and simmer 30 minutes. Stir often.

3. Fry veal in cooking oil about 10 minutes, until golden brown. Add water, salt and pepper and simmer 5 minutes.

   To serve: place veal over rice mixture and pour gravy over all.

Hot style sausage may be substituted for the sweet, according to taste.

veal cutlets and artichokes

1½ lbs. serrated veal shoulder steak
   cooking oil
1 pkg. frozen artichoke hearts,
   thawed, drained
½ clove garlic, minced
1 T lemon juice
¼ C dry vermouth
   lemon slices

1. Fry veal in cooking oil about 10 minutes, until golden brown. Remove to hot platter.

2. Add artichoke hearts and garlic to pan drippings and cook until browned. Arrange next to veal.

3. Add lemon juice and vermouth to pan. Bring to a boil and reduce by half. Pour over veal and artichokes. Garnish with lemon slices.

party veal casserole

12 serrated veal shoulder steaks
   cooking oil
 4 large potatoes, sliced thin
 2 onions, sliced
 ½ lb. mushrooms, sliced
12 slices eggplant, cut ⅜″ thick
1½ T margarine
 3 T flour
 2 C chicken broth
 1 C dry white wine
 2 T tomato paste
 2 T lemon juice
 ½ t salt
 ½ t basil
 ½ t dry mustard
 ½ t pepper
12 tomato slices
 2 pkg. frozen asparagus spears,
      thawed, drained
 6 T brandy

1. Saute separately in cooking oil and set aside: veal, potatoes, onions, mushrooms and eggplant.

2. Melt margarine; stir in flour and cook 2 minutes, stirring constantly. Gradually add broth and wine and cook until thick. Stir in tomato paste, lemon juice, salt, basil, mustard and pepper.

3. Layer the potatoes on the bottom of a baking dish. Place the veal over the potatoes. Do not overlap. Spread onions over all.

4. Spread mushrooms over the onions. Place a single layer of eggplant in the dish, placing 1 slice of eggplant over each veal steak to insure easy serving. Place a tomato slice on top of each eggplant slice. Arrange asparagus spears decoratively over all.

5. Spoon sauce over casserole. Bake in a 350° oven for 40 minutes.

6. Warm brandy, ignite and pour over casserole to serve.

A complete party meal with a wide selection of vegetables to please the most discriminating guest.

This company dish serves twelve.

cotes de veau en papillotes

 6 rib veal chops, boned
    cooking oil
½ lb. mushrooms, minced
 1 t shallots, minced
 1 T parsley, chopped
¼ t salt
 2 T margarine
 1 recipe Thick White Sauce
 6 pieces aluminum foil, 12x12″
12 slices smoked dark meat turkey

1. Saute the veal chops in cooking oil for 25 minutes or until golden brown on both sides.

2. Cook the mushrooms, shallots, parsley and salt in the margarine until all moisture disappears. Add the white sauce and mix thoroughly.

3. Arrange 6 stacks in the following order:
   1 piece foil
   1 slice turkey
   1 spoonful mushroom mixture
   1 chop
   1 spoonful mushroom mixture
   1 slice turkey

4. Draw up sides of foil and seal tightly.

5. Bake on a cookie sheet in a 400° oven for 6 minutes.

6. To serve, cut envelope partially open. Roll down flap to expose contents. Serve chops on individual plates. They are eaten from their foil cases.

For a more elegant presentation, envelopes may be fashioned from parchment paper. Grease the inside and bake until browned.

veal chops alla milanese

6 rib chops, cut very thin
1 egg, beaten
1½ C bread crumbs
3 T cooking oil
3 T olive oil
½ t salt
1 lemon, cut into wedges

1. Pound the meat on the chop very thin.

2. Dip the chops into the egg.

3. Press the bread crumbs into the meat.

4. Allow to stand 5 minutes.

5. Saute the chops in a mixture of the oils, until golden brown. Sprinkle with salt.

6. Serve with lemon wedges.

This dish is not complete without its garnish of lemon wedges.

thick white sauce

3 T margarine
3 T flour
1 C liquid non-dairy creamer
⅛ t white pepper
⅛ t nutmeg

Melt margarine; stir in flour and cook for 2 minutes, stirring constantly. Gradually add non-dairy creamer and seasonings and cook until thick.

veal chops with fresh tarragon

6 thick rib veal chops
   flour, mixed with salt and pepper
   cooking oil
6 sprigs fresh tarragon, chopped
⅓ C dry white wine
¾ C vegetable broth
1 beef bouillon cube

1. Rub the veal chops with the flour mixture.

2. Saute them slowly in cooking oil for 15 minutes on each side. Remove to hot platter.

3. Add the tarragon to the pan and deglaze with the wine. Add broth and bouillon cube and bring to a boil. Pour over veal chops.

Some of the best formed leaves of the tarragon sprigs may be reserved for garnish. Before using the leaves to decorate, blanch them in boiling water for one minute and then plunge them into cold water.

veal chops with olives

6 rib veal chops
½ C green olives, pitted
6 T cooking oil
3 T onion, minced
½ C smoked dark meat turkey, minced
½ clove garlic, minced

1. Cook the olives in boiling water for 3 minutes. Drain.

2. Brown the chops in the cooking oil. Add the onion and turkey. Cover and cook over low heat until tender.

3. Add the olives and the garlic and continue cooking an additional 5 minutes.

cherry veal chops

6 rib veal chops
1 lb. 6 oz. can cherry pie filling
½ C orange juice
3 T sherry
¼ t dry mustard
½ t ginger
3 T cooking oil
2 T grated orange peel

1. Strain cherry pie filling to separate cherries from sauce.

2. Combine pie filling sauce, orange juice, sherry, mustard and ginger. Set aside.

3. Brown chops on both sides in cooking oil. Pour off fat.

4. Pour sauce over chops. Cover and simmer 30 minutes, or until done. Stir occasionally to prevent scorching.

5. Add cherries to pan and cook 5 minutes more. Garnish with grated orange peel.

This dish is for those who like it sweet.

country style veal chops

4 veal chops, cut ½″ thick, either shoulder or rib
6 T cooking oil
4 onions, sliced
3 potatoes, sliced
½ t salt
½ t pepper

1. Brown veal chops in 2 tablespoons cooking oil. Remove to plate.

2. Saute onions and potatoes in 4 tablespoons cooking oil until onions are translucent.

3. Add veal chops, salt and pepper to the onions and potatoes; cover and simmer 45 minutes.

sicilian veal chops

4 shoulder veal chops
¼ lb. Italian olives
4 T olive oil
1 stalk celery, chopped
1 carrot, chopped
½ t capers
1 T mint
¼ C vinegar

1. Pound green olives gently to split, but do not break through into separate pieces. Pits do not have to be removed.

2. Saute the meat in olive oil for 35 minutes.

3. Add the celery, carrots and olives and saute until limp.

4. Add the remaining ingredients and saute 10 minutes.

5. Serve warm or cool, not hot.

The dish you'll wish you had made when your family is late for dinner.

veal and eggplant casserole

3 lbs. shoulder veal chops
   cooking oil
3 large eggplants, sliced ⅛" thick
2 recipes Italian Tomato Sauce I
   bread crumbs

1. Saute veal chops in a small amount of cooking oil until brown. Set aside.

2. Saute eggplant in cooking oil, drain on paper towels and set aside. Reserve oil.

3. To assemble: in a casserole layer sauce, eggplant, sauce, bread crumbs, veal chops. Now top with sauce, eggplant and sauce again.

4. Cover sauce with ¼ inch layer of bread crumbs. Sprinkle with oil used to saute eggplant.

5. Bake in a 350° oven for 45 minutes.

Eggplant absorbs a great quantity of oil, you might have to add more. Do be patient — as after it is absorbed, it is then released.

italian tomato sauce I

35 oz. can whole tomatoes
 4 T parsley, chopped
 4 T basil, chopped
 1 t garlic salt
 ½ t black pepper
 ¼ t crushed red pepper
 2 T olive oil
 1 onion, minced
 ½ t oregano
 1 T capers, packed in salt, rinsed
 1 t sugar

1. Combine all ingredients. Crush down tomatoes.

2. Boil quickly to reduce liquid. Cook to desired consistency.

This sauce may be used on pizza; or it may be combined with cooked vegetables, or with a combination of cooked vegetables and cooked meat.

mustard veal roast

3 lb. boneless chuck veal roast
1½ C dry white wine
⅓ C red wine vinegar
1 carrot, chopped
1 onion, chopped
½ t thyme
1 T parsley, chopped
2 bay leaves
½ t salt
½ t white pepper
4 T margarine, softened
2 t prepared mustard
⅓ C cooking oil

1. Marinate veal in wine, vinegar, carrot, onion, thyme, parsley, bay leaves, salt and pepper. Allow to stand overnight. Remove veal and pat dry. Reserve marinade.

2. Combine margarine and mustard. Spread over the veal. Roll and tie securely.

3. Brown meat in cooking oil. Add 1 cup marinade, cover and simmer 2 hours. Remove veal to serving platter.

4. Add balance of marinade to pan juices, bring to a boil and reduce by half. Strain and pour over meat.

veal pot roast

4 lb. boneless shoulder veal roast,
    or boneless chuck veal roast
1 T dry mustard
1 t poultry seasoning
1 T brown sugar
½ t salt
½ t white pepper
1 T flour
3 T cooking oil
1 onion, sliced
2 T white wine vinegar
¼ C water

1. Combine all dry ingredients and rub into the roast.

2. Brown meat in cooking oil.

3. Add onion, vinegar and water. Cover and simmer 2½ hours.

Meat may be rolled and tied if desired.

dilly veal roast

4 lb. boneless shoulder veal roast
   or boneless chuck veal roast
1 onion, chopped
   cooking oil
1 C water
1 bay leaf
4 potatoes, quartered
5 carrots, quartered
1 t salt
½ t white pepper
3 T flour dissolved in 3 T water
½ t dill
½ C non-dairy sour cream

1. Brown the veal and onions in cooking oil.

2. Place veal on a rack in a roasting pan.

3. Add the water, bay leaf, vegetables, salt and pepper. Cover and bake in a 325° oven for 2 hours.

4. Remove meat and vegetables to a serving plate.

5. Thicken pan juices with the flour mixture. Add the dill.

6. Stir in the non-dairy sour cream. Pour the sauce over the meat and vegetables, and serve.

vitello al pomidoro
veal with tomatoes

 4 lb. boneless shoulder veal roast,
    or boneless chuck veal roast
    cooking oil
18 small white onions
 8 carrots, cut into 2″ pieces
 1 T sugar
 1 clove garlic, crushed
 ½ C dry white wine
 4 tomatoes, chopped
 1 stalk celery, chopped
 4 sprigs parsley
 1 bay leaf
 ½ t thyme
 1 pkg. frozen green peas, thawed
 6 lettuce leaves, chopped

1. Brown the veal in cooking oil. Remove to plate.

2. Add onion, carrots, sugar and garlic and cook until brown.

3. Return the meat to the pan and add wine, tomatoes, celery, parsley, bay leaf and thyme.

4. Bring to a boil. Cover, reduce heat and simmer 2 hours.

5. Add the peas and lettuce and simmer 15 minutes.

vitello tonnato

3 lb. boneless shoulder of veal, rolled and tied
5 peppercorns
1 bay leaf
7 sprigs parsley
½ C dry white wine
1 onion
1 thick slice of lemon
3 T lemon juice
6 T tuna substitute
2½ T olive oil
2 T capers, packed in salt, not rinsed
1 t salt
2 C mayonnaise
   lemon, sliced thin
   minced capers
   minced parsley

1. Combine veal, peppercorns, bay leaf, parsley, wine, onion and lemon slice in saucepan. Cover, bring to a boil and simmer 1½ hours.

2. Remove meat from cooking liquid and chill meat over night. Reserve ½ cup of strained cooking liquid.

3. Put into blender or food processor the reserved broth, lemon juice, tuna substitute, olive oil, capers, salt and mayonnaise. Blend into a smooth sauce. Chill overnight.

4. Slice veal into ¼ inch slices.

5. Pour a little of the sauce in a serving dish. Place veal slices over sauce and cover with remaining sauce. Refrigerate until serving time.

6. Garnish with thin slices of lemon and sprinkle with parsley and capers.

This classical veal dish is traditionally prepared with tuna fish. We have located at least one fish substitute in a vegetarian food store. This dish can now be included in your gourmet recipe file.

cima di vitello
cold stuffed breast of veal in aspic

1 breast of veal with pocket, boned; reserve bones
⅓ C onion, minced
1 clove garlic, minced
1 T cooking oil
8 oz. veal, ground
¼ lb. calves liver, ground
¾ C bread crumbs
2 eggs
¼ C brandy
1 t salt
1 t basil
¾ t thyme
¼ t allspice
¼ t ginger
¼ t pepper
4 T cooking oil
1 carrot, sliced
1 onion, sliced
½ t thyme
2 C chicken broth
1 bay leaf

1. Saute the onion and garlic in cooking oil until limp. Place in a bowl and combine with ground veal, ground liver, bread crumbs, eggs, brandy, salt, basil, thyme, allspice, ginger and pepper.

2. Stuff this mixture into the pocket in veal breast; sew together to encase stuffing.

3. Brown the veal in the cooking oil.

4. Place the veal, carrots, onion, thyme, chicken broth, bay leaf and reserved bones in a casserole. Bake, covered, in a 350° oven for 2 hours. Remove veal to plate and refrigerate. Strain stock into a bowl and refrigerate overnight.

5. The next day, slice meat and arrange on serving dish.

6. Remove fat from stock and heat. Pour stock over meat. Return to refrigerator and chill to set, about 20 minutes.

stuffed breast of veal

1 breast of veal
1 recipe Stuffing for veal
  garlic salt
  thyme
  paprika
  cooking oil
½ C beef broth
½ C dry white wine

1. Ask your butcher to prepare the breast of veal: create a pocket suitable for stuffing; crack the breast bones; cut through the cartilage (to facilitate slicing at serving time).
2. Prepare stuffing according to recipe.
3. Stuff the pocket in the breast.
4. Cover the open end of the stuffing with 2 pieces of doubled aluminum foil. Secure it with skewers, or sew it.
5. Rub the veal with garlic salt, thyme and paprika.
6. Sear the veal in oil until browned.
7. Place in a roasting pan. Add the beef broth and wine. Cover.
8. Roast in a 325° oven for 20 minutes to the pound. Baste often. Remove cover for the last 30 minutes.

It is always best to use a meat thermometer. The reading should be 170° when done.

fruit stuffing

3 C bread cubes
½ C golden raisins
1½ C tart apples, chopped
1 t grated orange peel
2 T onion, minced
¾ t celery seed
1 t marjoram
3 T margarine, melted
1 t salt

Combine all ingredients and use to stuff veal pocket.

stuffing supreme

1 onion, chopped
2 cloves garlic, chopped
   cooking oil
¼ lb. cooked tongue
¼ lb. veal
¼ lb. smoked dark meat turkey
1 C bread crumbs
2 t basil
½ t hot sauce
¼ t nutmeg
1 t ginger
½ C parsley, chopped
½ t salt
1 t pepper
2 eggs
½ C dry white wine

1. Saute onion and garlic in cooking oil, until onion is limp.

2. Grind together the tongue, veal and turkey.

3. Combine onion mixture, ground meats and all remaining ingredients.

4. Use to stuff veal pocket.

beef and rice stuffing

½ lb. ground beef
½ C cooked rice
¼ C parsley, chopped
1 clove garlic, minced
2 stalks celery, chopped
1 onion, chopped
   cooking oil
1 egg
½ t salt
½ t pepper

1. Saute garlic, onion, celery and parsley in cooking oil until limp.

2. Combine all ingredients and use to stuff veal pocket.

oriental stuffing

4 Chinese mushrooms
½ C onion, minced
1 T cooking oil
2 C potatoes, grated
1 t salt
2 T potato starch
1 egg
1 t caraway seeds
½ t white pepper

1. Soak mushrooms in hot water for 30 minutes. Squeeze out water. Remove stems and discard. Mince mushrooms.

2. Saute onion in cooking oil until limp.

3. Combine all ingredients and use to stuff veal pocket.

florentine stuffing

3 T onion, minced
½ lb. sweet kosher Italian sausage, casing removed
2 pkgs. frozen chopped spinach, thawed, squeezed
1 C bread crumbs
3 eggs
1 t salt
½ t white pepper

1. Brown onions and sausage meat together.

2. Mix all ingredients together and use to stuff veal pocket.

italian breast of veal

1 breast of veal with pocket, boned;
   reserve bones
3 slices bread, crusts removed
⅔ C liquid non-dairy creamer
½ C onions, chopped
2 T margarine
¼ lb. chicken, ground
¼ lb. veal, ground
1 sweetbread, blanched 10 mins.,
   skinned, finely chopped
½ C frozen spinach, thawed, squeezed
2 T parsley, chopped
¼ t marjoram
¼ t thyme
1 t salt
1 egg
½ C pistachio nuts
1 C peas
3 hard cooked eggs, whole
1 onion
3 cloves garlic
1 carrot
1 bay leaf
2 sprigs parsley
8 C chicken broth
2 C dry white wine
¼ t white pepper

1. Soak bread in non-dairy creamer.

2. Saute onions in margarine until limp.

3. In a bowl combine onions, chicken, ground veal, sweetbread, spinach, parsley, majoram, thyme, salt and egg.

4. Squeeze out the excess liquid from the bread and mix into the bowl.

5. Fold in pistachio nuts and peas.

6. Spread half of the stuffing into bottom of veal pocket. Arrange hard cooked eggs lengthwise in a row. Spoon in remaining stuffing over the eggs. Sew up opening.

7. Put veal bones and onion, garlic, carrot, bay leaf and parsley in a large pot. Place the veal on top. Add broth and wine to cover the meat. Add pepper and bring to a boil.

8. Reduce heat, cover and simmer 1¼ hours.

9. Remove meat to a dish, and refrigerate until chilled.

10. Cut into ¼ inch slices and serve cold.

Yellow and white daisies, used as a centerpiece, reflect the slices of egg in the stuffing. A pretty summer dish!

rolled breast of veal

1 breast of veal, boned, butterflied,
    pounded thin
1 carrot, minced
1 shallot, minced
¼ C celery, minced
    cooking oil
4 oz. tofu
1 egg yolk
2 T garlic salt
¼ lb. smoked dark meat turkey,
    minced
3 slices bologna, minced
1 hard cooked egg, minced
½ t sage
4 T parsley, minced
4 T olive oil
1 T rosemary
1 C dry white wine
1 C chicken broth

1. Saute carrots, shallots and celery in cooking oil.
2. Blend the tofu, egg yolk and garlic salt to make a paste.
3. Combine turkey, bologna, tofu mixture, carrot mixture, egg, sage and parsley; spread over meat.
4. Roll and tie securely.
5. Brown meat in olive oil. Add rosemary, wine and broth.
6. Cover and simmer 1½ hours.

Tofu is a neutral tasting product made of soybeans. Make your own or buy it fresh at natural food stores. It is also available canned and as a dry mix.

veau oeufs brouilles
cold stuffed breast of veal with eggs

1 breast of veal, boned, butterflied
¼ lb. smoked dark meat turkey, cut
    very thin
7 eggs
½ t salt
½ t white pepper
2 T margarine
¼ C parsley, minced
¼ C chives, minced
4 T cooking oil
1 carrot, sliced
2 shallots, sliced
1 stalk celery, chopped

1. Pound veal very thin and evenly between 2 pieces of waxed paper.

2. Cover veal with smoked turkey.

3. Combine eggs with salt and pepper. Scramble eggs in 2 tablespoons melted margarine. Cool.

4. Spread egg mixture over the turkey. Sprinkle with parsley and chives.

5. Roll up tightly and secure with string. Sew ends closed.

6. Brown meat in cooking oil. Remove to plate. Place remaining ingredients in roasting pan. Place veal on top of vegetables.

7. Bake, uncovered, in a 325° oven for 2½ hours, basting often.

8. Chill thoroughly. Slice before serving.

It is advisable to use a meat thermometer with this dish. Reading should be 170°.

hungarian veal roll

1 breast of veal, boned, butterflied,
    pounded thin
   flour
2 slices bread
¼ C liquid non-dairy creamer
½ lb. mushrooms
3 chicken livers
2 egg yolks
1 T parsley, chopped
1 T green pepper, chopped
1 T onion, chopped
½ t grated lemon peel
½ t salt
¾ t paprika
⅛ t cayenne pepper
4 T sweet white wine
2 T margarine
2 C non-dairy sour cream
½ C chicken broth

1. Dredge veal in flour.

2. Soak bread in non-dairy creamer.

3. Grind together mushrooms, bread and chicken livers.

4. Combine ground mixture with egg yolks, parsley, pepper, onion, lemon peel, salt, paprika, cayenne and wine.

5. Cook this mixture in margarine for 5 minutes. Cool.

6. Spread mixture over veal. Roll and tie securely.

7. Brown in cooking oil. Remove to baking dish.

8. Gently warm the non-dairy sour cream and chicken broth together. Then bring to a boil.

9. Pour over meat, cover tightly and bake in a 325° oven for 1 hour. Turn meat, cover and continue to bake an additional hour.

veal riblets marengo

    1 breast of veal, cut into ribs
       flour
    1 onion, minced
    2 cloves garlic, minced
   ⅓ C oil
    1 C canned tomatoes, chopped
    3 T parsley, chopped
 1½ C vegetable stock
    4 T tomato paste
    1 C dry white wine
    1 jar white onions, browned in
          margarine
   12 mushroom caps, browned in
          margarine
   ½ t lemon juice

1. Dredge veal in flour.

2. Saute the onion and garlic in oil until limp.

3. Add the meat and brown well.

4. Add the tomatoes, parsley, stock, tomato paste and wine. Bring to a boil.

5. Cover, reduce heat and simmer for 1½ hours.

6. Remove meat to serving platter, arrange with onions and mushrooms.

7. Skim fat off sauce remaining in pan. Add lemon juice.

8. Cook sauce rapidly to reduce by half. Pour sauce over meat and vegetables.

Veal riblets are not to be overlooked; meat surrounding bones is always the tastiest.

herbed veal riblets

1 breast of veal, cut into ribs
flour
2 C onions, sliced
2 T olive oil
2 T grated orange peel
2 t rosemary
1 t basil
½ t garlic, minced
1 bay leaf
⅔ C dry vermouth
⅔ C water

1. Dredge veal in flour.
2. Place ribs on broiler pan on lowest rack in oven; cook for 30 minutes on broil temperature. Turn often. Remove to casserole.
3. Combine remaining ingredients and bring to a boil.
4. Add this mixture to the ribs. Bake, covered, in a 350° oven for 1½ hours, basting frequently.

marinated veal riblets

1 breast of veal, cut into ribs
1 C orange juice
1 onion, sliced
2 T oil
1 t salt
2 t coriander
1 t garlic, minced
1 t cumin
1 t oregano
½ t crushed red pepper
¼ t cinnamon

1. Combine all ingredients, except meat, to make a marinade. Marinate the veal ribs for 6 hours.
2. Place veal and marinade in a roasting pan large enough to hold the ribs in one layer. Cover very tightly with foil.
3. Bake in a 350° oven for 45 minutes.
4. Uncover and continue to bake 1 hour, basting frequently.

osso bucco

3 lbs. meaty veal shanks, cut into
    2″ pieces
2 T cooking oil
1 C onion, diced
½ C celery, diced
¾ C carrots, diced
2 T parsley, chopped
1 clove garlic, minced
1 T tomato paste
2 tomatoes, chopped
1 C dry white wine
1 C chicken broth
½ t salt
½ t pepper
½ t rosemary
1 recipe Gremalata

1. Brown veal in cooking oil. Remove veal to a warm plate.

2. To the same oil, add onions, celery, carrots and parsley; saute for 5 minutes.

3. Add garlic, tomato paste and tomatoes. Stir to blend.

4. Add wine, broth, salt, pepper and rosemary. Blend well.

5. Return veal to pan and place in a single layer. Bring to a boil. Cover, reduce heat, and simmer 2 hours.

6. To serve: arrange the veal shanks on a serving platter; pour the sauce over all. Garnish with **Gremalata.**

Antique buffs take note: start a collection of marrow picks to serve with this dish.

gremalata

2 t grated lemon peel
1 clove garlic, minced
3 T parsley, chopped

Combine all ingredients.

blanquette de veau

2 lbs. boneless veal for stewing, cut
    into cubes
4 carrots, cut into ½" pieces
1 stalk celery, cut into ½" pieces
2 onions, studded with 4 cloves
2 leeks, cut into 1" pieces
1 bay leaf
¼ t thyme
2 sprigs parsley
¾ C dry vermouth
1 T margarine
1 T flour
¼ t nutmeg
½ C liquid non-dairy creamer
2 egg yolks
1 jar white onions, browned in
    margarine
½ lb. mushroom caps, sauteed

1. Place veal in a deep saucepan and cover with water. Bring to a boil and skim.

2. Add carrots, celery, onions, leeks, bay leaf, thyme, parsley and vermouth; cover and cook slowly for 1 hour.

3. Melt margarine and add flour and nutmeg. Strain veal broth into pan and continue to cook for 15 minutes, stirring occasionally.

4. Combine non-dairy creamer and egg yolks in a bowl. Add a little of the hot mixture and then return the tempered mixture to the pan.

5. Arrange meat, onions and mushrooms in a serving tureen. Pour sauce over all.

A blanquette is a white stew, made with either veal or chicken.

veal pie

3 lbs. boneless veal for stewing, cut into cubes
1 onion, stuck with 2 cloves
1 carrot, sliced
4 slices lemon
1 bay leaf
½ t thyme
½ t salt
½ t pepper
5 T margarine
5 T flour
2 egg yolks
½ C liquid non-dairy creamer
½ t nutmeg
2 T capers
1 recipe Flakey Pastry

1. Cover meat with water, bring to a boil and simmer 5 minutes. Drain.

2. Cover meat again with water, bring to a boil and add onion, carrot, lemon slices, bay leaf, thyme, salt and pepper. Simmer 1 hour. Remove meat. Strain and reserve cooking liquid.

3. Melt margarine; stir in flour and cook for 2 minutes, stirring constantly. Gradually add 3½ cups of strained broth from the veal and cook until thick.

4. Combine egg yolks, non-dairy creamer and nutmeg. Gradually add this to the thickened sauce.

5. Place meat in a casserole, pour in sauce; add capers. Cover with a layer of pastry. Vent pastry.

6. Bake in a 425° oven for 20 minutes.

Leftover **Blanquette de Veau** *can be used as the base of this recipe.*

mediterranean veal stew

3 lbs. boneless veal for stewing, cut
      into cubes
   flour
   salt
   white pepper
4 T olive oil
½ C onions, chopped
½ C sweet white wine
2 T tomato paste
2 T margarine
½ lb. mushrooms, sliced
2 T liquid non-dairy creamer

1. Toss veal in a mixture of flour, salt and pepper.

2. Brown veal and onions in oil.

3. Add wine and tomato paste; cover and cook over low heat for 1 hour.

4. In another pan, saute mushrooms in margarine until soft. Add non-dairy creamer and mix well.

5. Add mushroom mixture to meat. Cook an additional 5 minutes and serve.

Steps 1, 2 and 3 may be done the day before. At serving time, bring to a boil and proceed with steps 4 and 5.

peruvian veal

2 lbs. boneless veal for stewing, cut into cubes
1 onion, chopped
1 clove garlic, minced
  cooking oil
  flour
3 C chicken broth
2 C canned tomatoes
½ C peanut butter
½ t salt
½ t pepper
1 pkg. frozen carrots, thawed, drained
1 pkg. frozen peas, thawed, drained

1. Cook onion and garlic in cooking oil until translucent.

2. Dust veal with flour and brown lightly.

3. Add broth, tomatoes, peanut butter, salt and pepper. Cover and simmer for 1 hour.

4. Add vegetables and simmer an additional 15 minutes.

haitian veal stew

2 lbs. boneless veal for stewing, cut into cubes
3 T cooking oil
1 t flour
2 t white pepper
1½ cloves garlic, minced
1 T Worcestershire sauce
8 oz. can tomato sauce
¾ C salted cashew nuts
1½ C water

1. Brown veal on all sides in cooking oil.

2. Combine all ingredients. Bring to a boil. Reduce heat, cover, and simmer 1 hour.

Caution: gradually add the pepper to your own taste.

hunter style veal

2 lbs. boneless veal for stewing, cut into cubes
½ lb. green Italian olives
1 onion, minced
¼ t thyme
1 bay leaf
½ t salt
½ t white pepper
1 C dry white wine
3 T cooking oil
1 C carrot, minced
¼ C celery, minced
1 T dried mint
¼ t crushed red pepper
¼ C wine vinegar
½ C dry vermouth

1. Pound green olives gently to split, but do not break through into separate pieces. Pits do not have to be removed.

2. Place veal, onion, thyme, bay leaf and wine in a bowl. Cover and marinate overnight. Drain and reserve marinade.

3. Brown meat in cooking oil. Add carrots, celery, mint, olives, salt and pepper and ½ cup marinade. Cover and simmer 45 minutes.

4. Add vinegar and vermouth. Bring to a boil. Do not cover. Boil 5 minutes. Cool to room temperature and serve.

It is best served warm, not hot.

hungarian goulash

1 lb. boneless veal for stewing, cut into cubes
1 lb. boneless beef for stewing, cut into cubes
  flour
  cooking oil
1 large onion, chopped
1 T paprika
8 oz. can tomato sauce
4 potatoes, quartered

1. Lightly flour meat. Brown meat in cooking oil.

2. Add onions and cook until transparent. Add paprika and cook 2 minutes.

3. Add tomato sauce and cook 1 hour.

4. Add potatoes and cook an additional 30 minutes.

The combination of beef and veal in this dish gives latitude to your meal planning; use the combination in any proportion.

veal paprika

2 lb. boneless veal for stewing, cut into cubes
¼ C cooking oil
¼ C onions, chopped
½ t salt
1 T paprika
1 T parsley, minced
1½ C water
½ lb. mushrooms, sliced, sauteed
1 C non-dairy sour cream

1. Brown veal in cooking oil. Add onions, salt, paprika, parsley and water. Cover and simmer 45 minutes.

2. Add mushrooms to the veal. Cook an additional 15 minutes.

3. Slowly stir in non-dairy sour cream.

If you prefer a thicker sauce, combine 2 T water and 2 T flour. Stir into sauce to thicken.

This dish goes particularly well with hot, wide noodles.

veal ragout

2 lbs. boneless veal for stewing, cut into cubes
2 T flour
¼ C olive oil
1½ C onions, chopped
1 clove garlic, minced
½ C chicken broth
½ C beef broth
1 C dry white wine
1 T tomato paste
1½ C canned tomatoes, chopped
½ t salt
½ t thyme
½ t savory
½ lb. mushrooms, sliced, sauteed
½ C oil cured black olives, pitted

1. Dredge meat in flour. Brown veal in olive oil. Remove meat to a casserole.

2. Saute onions and garlic until limp. Add liquids, tomato paste, tomatoes and seasonings. Bring to a boil.

3. Pour this mixture over the meat and bake in a 325° oven for 2 hours.

4. Add the mushrooms and olives and cook an additional 20 minutes.

sweet and sour veal stew

3 lbs. boneless veal for stewing, cut into cubes
2 T flour
¼ C cooking oil
2 C onions, chopped
1 C tomatoes, chopped
¾ C beef broth
½ C raisins
¼ C lemon juice
3 T sugar
½ t ginger
½ t salt
½ t cinnamon
½ t white pepper

1. Dredge veal in flour; brown in cooking oil and place in a casserole.

2. Add onions to skillet and saute until limp. Add remaining ingredients and bring to a boil.

3. Pour this mixture into the casserole, over and around the veal; bake in a 325° oven for 2 hours.

A definite change of pace.

spezzatino di vitello

veal stew

1½ lbs. boneless veal for stewing, cut
    into cubes
 3 T olive oil
 ½ clove garlic
    flour
 1 t salt
 ½ t white pepper
 1 T parsley, minced
 1 C dry white wine
1½ C canned tomatoes, chopped
 1 package frozen peas, thawed,
    drained

1. Saute the garlic in olive oil until golden. Discard garlic.

2. Dredge veal in flour. Brown meat in seasoned olive oil.

3. Add remaining ingredients, except peas. Bring to a boil. Add water to barely cover meat, if needed.

4. Cover and simmer for 1 hour, adding additional liquid if needed.

5. Add peas, bring to a boil and serve hot.

vitella con peperoni

veal with peppers

1½ lbs. boneless veal for stewing, cut
    into cubes
 1 onion, sliced
 4 Italian peppers, cut into strips
 6 T olive oil
2½ C canned tomatoes, chopped
 ½ t salt
 ¼ t white pepper
 ⅔ C dry white wine

1. Saute onions and peppers in olive oil until tender. Set aside.

2. Brown veal in skillet, adding more oil if necessary.

3. Add tomatoes, salt and pepper. Cover and simmer 1 hour.

4. Add wine, and the onions and peppers. Cover and simmer an additional 15 minutes.

Use only Italian peppers, red or green, not the bell variety. Frozen Italian peppers can be used successfully.

basic veal and tomato stew

1½ lbs. boneless veal for stewing, cut into cubes
cooking oil
1 onion, chopped
1 clove garlic, minced
1 T flour
2 C chicken broth
1 C canned tomatoes
1 t lemon juice
¼ t oregano
¼ t salt
¼ t white pepper
12 mushrooms, sliced

1. Brown the veal on all sides in the cooking oil.
2. Add onions and garlic and saute until translucent.
3. Combine flour, broth, tomatoes, lemon juice and seasonings. Bring to a boil and pour over veal and onions.
4. Cover and simmer gently for one hour.
5. Add mushrooms and cook ½ hour more.

easy veal stew

1½ lbs. boneless veal for stewing, cut into cubes
1 C bread crumbs
1 C dry white wine
1 C beef broth
1 clove garlic, chopped
1 onion, chopped
2 T parsley, minced
½ t thyme
½ t salt
¼ t white pepper
⅛ t cloves

1. Do not brown meat. Combine all ingredients in a casserole.
2. Bake in a 350° oven for 1 hour.

Garnish with chopped chives.

simple curried veal

2 lbs. boneless veal for stewing, cut
   into cubes
   cooking oil
1 onion, chopped
1 t sugar
1 t curry powder
3 T flour
1 t salt
¼ t pepper
¼ t paprika
¼ t dry mustard
   boiling water to cover meat
½ C non-dairy sour cream

1. Brown meat in cooking oil.

2. Add onions and brown.

3. Add sugar, curry, flour and seasonings.
   Stir and cook until flour is absorbed.

4. Add boiling water and simmer for 1½
   hours.

5. Remove from heat and stir in non-dairy
   sour cream.

*In a hurry? Want something different? Try
this one.*

veal pojarsky

1½ lbs. veal, ground very fine
  1 C bread cubes
  1 C liquid non-dairy creamer
  1 egg white
  ⅓ C margarine, melted
  1 t salt
  ½ t pepper
  ½ t nutmeg
  ½ C bread crumbs
  ½ C margarine

1. Soak bread cubes in non-dairy creamer for 10 minutes. Squeeze out and reserve excess liquid.

2. Combine veal, soaked bread, egg white, remaining non-dairy creamer, melted margarine, salt, pepper and nutmeg. Mix thoroughly to a paste-like consistency.

3. Divide mixture into 6 portions and shape into flat cutlets.

4. Press into bread crumbs.

5. Saute in margarine until golden brown on all sides.

Step 2 is best accomplished in a food processor or in an electric mixer on high speed.

Pojarsky are made with white meat, veal or chicken; **Bitoques** *with beef.*

veal balls in lemon sauce

1 lb. ground veal
¾ C bread crumbs
1 egg
1 T parsley, chopped
¼ t salt
½ t white pepper
⅔ t nutmeg
⅓ C liquid non-dairy creamer
   flour
   cooking oil
1 recipe Lemon Sauce

1. Combine first 8 ingredients.
2. Form into small balls. Roll in flour.
3. Brown the balls in cooking oil. Cover, reduce heat and cook, stirring occasionally, for 20 minutes.
4. Serve with **Lemon Sauce**.

lemon sauce

2 egg yolks
3 T lemon juice
2 T cornstarch
2 C chicken broth

1. Combine egg yolks and lemon juice. Set aside.
2. Combine cornstarch with ½ cup chicken broth. Set aside.
3. Bring remaining chicken broth to a boil. Add cornstarch mixture and cook until thick.
4. Remove from heat and cool. Add egg yolk mixture slowly, stirring constantly.
5. Place over boiling water and cook, stirring constantly, until thickened.

sauerbraten veal patties

  2 lbs. ground veal
  1 onion, minced
  ¾ C bread crumbs
  3 eggs
  ½ t salt
     cooking oil
  ½ C red wine vinegar
1½ C water
  1 t cloves
  2 bay leaves
  ⅓ C gingersnap crumbs

1. Mix together the veal, onion, bread crumbs, eggs and salt. Form into patties.

2. Brown patties on both sides in cooking oil.

3. Add vinegar, water and seasonings. Cover and simmer gently for 45 minutes.

4. Add gingersnaps to thicken and continue cooking an additional 15 minutes.

German Red Cabbage *or* **Prunes and Onions** *round out this Central European-style dish.*

tangy veal patties

  2 lbs. ground veal
  ½ t salt
  ½ t pepper
  3 T cooking oil
  ½ lb. mushrooms, sliced
  3 T flour
10 oz. beef broth
  ½ C dry white wine
  2 T lemon juice
  3 T capers
     lemon slices

1. Season the veal with salt and pepper. Form into patties.

2. Brown the patties in the cooking oil. Add the mushrooms and continue to cook until mushrooms are limp.

3. Stir in the flour.

4. Add the broth and cook until thick.

5. Add wine, lemon juice and capers. Cover and simmer 15 minutes.

6. Garnish with lemon slices and serve.

veal loaf

1½ lbs. ground veal
 ½ lb. smoked dark meat turkey,
      minced
 ¾ C bread crumbs
 ½ t salt
  2 T parsley, minced
  1 T onion, minced
 ¼ t sage
 ⅛ t ground cloves
 ⅛ t allspice
  1 egg

1. Mix together all ingredients.

2. Pack firmly into a greased loaf pan.

3. Bake in 350° oven for 1 hour.

4. Remove from loaf pan and chill. Slice and serve cold.

Something different for those endless school sandwiches.

veal hash

2 C cooked veal
1 onion
1 potato, boiled
¼ C green pepper
½ C liquid non-dairy creamer
3 T parsley, chopped
2 t vinegar
½ t white pepper
½ t garlic salt
  cooking oil

1. Grind together the veal, onion, potato and pepper.
2. Add all remaining ingredients, except the cooking oil.
3. Heat oil in a heavy skillet. Add the hash mixture and pack down. Cook until a crust is formed. Turn and cook on the other side until crusty.

Lemon juice may be substituted for the vinegar.

veal cakes

1 lb. cooked veal, minced
½ C onion, chopped
  cooking oil
3 cooked potatoes, mashed
1 egg, beaten
1 T parsley, chopped
¼ t salt
¼ t pepper
  flour
  cooking oil

1. Saute onions until limp. Combine with veal, potatoes, egg, parsley, salt and pepper. Mix well.
2. Form into cakes and roll in flour.
3. Brown cakes on both sides in cooking oil.

veal croquettes

2 C cooked veal, minced
3 T margarine
3 T flour
1 C liquid non-dairy creamer
2 T shallots, minced
2 t parsley, chopped
2 t tarragon
¼ t salt
¼ t white pepper
1 egg
1 T sherry
1 egg beaten with 1 T water
   bread crumbs
   cooking oil

1. Melt margarine; stir in flour and cook for 2 minutes, stirring constantly. Gradually add the non-dairy creamer and cook until thick.

2. Add the veal, shallots, parsley, spices, one egg and sherry. Continue cooking, stirring constantly, until the mixture thickens. Remove and chill.

3. Shape into croquettes. Dip into the bread crumbs, then into the beaten egg mixture, then into the crumbs again.

4. Return to refrigerator for 30 minutes.

5. Fry in cooking oil until golden brown.

Turn your leftover roast into croquettes, hash or cakes.

baked sausages and peppers

2 lbs. kosher Italian sausage, cut into 3″ pieces
1 lb. Italian peppers, sliced
3 onions, sliced
   cooking oil
1 recipe Italian Tomato Sauce I
½ t salt

1. Fry peppers and onions in cooking oil until limp.

2. In a clean pan, fry sausages until browned.

3. Combine all ingredients in a casserole and bake in a 350° oven for 30 minutes.

Kosher Italian sausage is a relatively new product. Made with Italian spices and veal, or a combination of veal and beef, it tastes exactly like its counterpart.

sausages, potatoes, peppers and onions

2 lbs. kosher Italian sausage, cut into 3″ pieces
4 potatoes, sliced
1 lb. Italian peppers, sliced
3 onions, sliced
   cooking oil
1 t salt

1. Fry potatoes, peppers and onions in cooking oil until all are cooked through and lightly browned. Sprinkle with salt.

2. Add sausages and continue to cook an additional 10 minutes.

sausage with savoy cabbage

  2 lbs. kosher Italian sausage
  2 C dry red wine
  1 clove garlic, minced
  ½ C onion, minced
 16 oz. can stewed tomatoes
  1 C water
  1 head savoy cabbage, coarsely
       chopped
  ½ t salt
  ½ t pepper

1. Prick sausages with a fork; cut into 3 inch pieces.

2. Combine sausage, wine and garlic. Marinate 30 minutes. Drain sausage and reserve marinade.

3. Fry sausage and onion until brown. Add marinade, cover and simmer 20 minutes.

4. Stir in undrained tomatoes, water and cabbage. Cover and simmer an additional 20 minutes. Add salt and pepper.

rack of lamb persille

1   rack of lamb
     margarine, softened
     pepper
¾   C bread crumbs
1   clove garlic, minced
¼   C parsley, minced
3   T olive oil

1. Ask your butcher to prepare the rack of lamb: crack the chine bone; French the ribs.

2. Rub the meat well with margarine and pepper. Wrap the ends of the bones with foil.

3. Combine bread crumbs, garlic, parsley and olive oil.

4. Place lamb, rib side down, on a rack in a roasting pan. Roast in a 400° oven for 35 minutes. Remove from oven and raise temperature to 500°.

5. Pat the crumb mixture onto the top of the rack. Return to oven until crumbs and rack are done, about 8 minutes. Lamb should be served pink on the inside; if used, the thermometer should register 145°.

6. Replace foil with paper frills; serve two.

Rack of lamb is one of the measures of excellence in a fine French restaurant, however it is not difficult to prepare. It is a costly dish, certainly not a hearty one; but it is one of the most elegant lamb dishes for the kosher table.

crown roast of lamb

2 **racks of lamb**
   cooking oil
   pepper
   tarragon
   garlic salt

1. Ask your butcher to prepare the racks: set them upright; tie them back to form a circle; French the ribs. (If he fills the center with ground lamb, remove it and reserve it for another dish.)

2. Rub the racks well with oil, pepper, tarragon and garlic salt. Wrap the tips of the bones with foil to prevent charring.

3. Place the crown on a rack in a shallow roasting pan.

4. Place a ball of crumpled foil in the center of the crown, filling the middle completely.

5. Roast in a 325° oven, 30 to 35 minutes per pound for well done; 12 to 15 minutes per pound for pink. Baste every 10 minutes.

6. Remove the crumpled foil and place the roast on a serving platter. Replace the foil on the tips of the bones with paper frills.

The center of a Crown Roast is very often stuffed with a filling before being served. However, to facilitate carving, our preference is to surround it with vegetables and serve it unfilled.

Bernaise Sauce *often accompanies this dish.*

bernaise sauce

  1 **C margarine**
 ¼ **C tarragon vinegar**
  4 **egg yolks**
  2 **T lemon juice**
 ¼ **t salt**
 ½ **t dry mustard**
  1 **T dry red wine**
  1 **shallot**
1½ **t tarragon**

1. Melt the margarine and vinegar together to just below the boiling point.

2. Place remaining ingredients in blender. Blend 30 seconds.

3. With the blender on, pour the hot, melted margarine into the container in a slow, steady stream. Serve warm.

party chops in pastry

6 rib lamb chops
cooking oil
¼ lb. mushrooms, minced
2 T onion, minced
2 T shallots, minced
salt
pepper
⅛ t lemon juice
1 recipe Flakey Pastry
12 thin slices smoked dark meat
   turkey
1 egg yolk mixed with 1 T water

1. French the lamb chops by scraping all the meat and fat from the top portion of the bone.

2. Brown lamb chops in cooking oil 4 minutes on each side. Remove from skillet and pat dry.

3. Saute mushrooms, onion and shallots in cooking oil until all moisture has evaporated. Add salt, pepper and lemon juice.

4. Roll out pastry and cut into 6 pieces, each piece large enough to encase one chop.

5. Place a slice of smoked dark meat turkey on pastry. Top with a tablespoon of the mushroom mixture and a lamb chop. Top this with more mushroom mixture and another slice of turkey.

6. Enclose the chop in the pastry, leaving the trimmed bone exposed. Wrap foil around the bone to prevent charring. Brush dough with egg yolk mixture.

7. Bake on a cookie sheet in a 400° oven for 30 minutes, or until pastry is lightly browned.

8. Replace foil with paper frills and serve.

savory stuffed lamb chops

6 rib lamb chops, cut 2″ thick
½ onion, minced
½ stalk celery, minced
½ clove garlic, minced
¼ C mushrooms, minced
2 T cooking oil
¾ C bread crumbs
½ t rosemary
2 T parsley, minced
¼ t salt
¼ t pepper

1. Saute the onion, celery, garlic and mushrooms in the cooking oil until the onion is limp.

2. Add the bread crumbs and seasonings and blend thoroughly.

3. Remove bone and outer skin from chops; discard. Make a horizontal slit in the meat; insert the stuffing. Draw end of chop around, forming a round flat piece. Secure with kitchen twine. Remove to broiler rack.

4. Place under broiler and brown both sides. Lower broiler rack; continue broiling, turning often, to desired state of doneness.

piccadilly lamb chops

6 rib lamb chops
1 T margarine
1 T flour
1½ C chicken broth
1 T margarine, melted
1 T parsley
1½ T red wine vinegar
½ onion, minced
1½ T dill pickle, minced

1. Melt margarine, stir in flour and cook for 2 minutes, stirring constantly. Gradually add broth and cook until thick. Set aside.

2. Combine melted margarine, parsley, vinegar and onion. Add to reserved sauce, blend well and bring to just below boiling point. Stir in pickle. Place sauce over low heat to keep warm.

3. Broil lamb chops to desired state of doneness. Pour sauce over chops and serve.

lamb chops español

8 rib lamb chops
4 T margarine
½ t tarragon
1 t mustard
¼ t pepper
3 T dry white wine
¼ C liquid non-dairy creamer
10 ripe olives, chopped

1. Broil chops to desired state of doneness. Reserve pan drippings.

2. Melt margarine, add tarragon, mustard, and pepper. Stir well. Add pan drippings and wine.

3. Add liquid non-dairy creamer and olives. Continue cooking 2 additional minutes. Pour sauce over chops and serve.

Make a small slit along the bone to determine the state of doneness. Rare lamb will be rosy; medium will be pink, and well done, a greyish brown.

breaded lamb chops

8 rib lamb chops
1 egg
1 T olive oil
  pepper
  flour
  bread crumbs
  cooking oil

1. Beat egg and olive oil together.

2. Sprinkle chops with pepper. Dust lightly with flour.

3. Dip chops into beaten egg mixture.

4. Press into bread crumbs.

5. Saute in cooking oil for about 8 minutes on each side.

Use rib chops (either plain, double or Frenched), noisettes (the trimmed eye of the rib), or shoulder chops. Regulate the cooking time according to the chops used.

Broiled peach halves filled with mint jelly are a nice accompaniment.

skillet lamb chops

6 shoulder lamb chops
4 T margarine
2 C catsup
2 T currant jelly
4 T sweet white wine
1 onion, minced
¼ t pepper
½ C mushrooms, sauteed

1. Combine the margarine, catsup, jelly, wine, onions, and pepper in a skillet. Bring to a boil.
2. Add the chops and simmer, uncovered, for 1 hour.
3. Add the mushrooms and continue simmering an additional 15 minutes.

lamb chops in white wine

6 shoulder lamb chops
   garlic salt
   pepper
   cooking oil
1 onion, chopped
6 shallots, chopped
1 T parsley, chopped
1 T flour
1 C dry white wine

1. Sprinkle the chops with garlic salt and pepper. Brown on both sides in cooking oil. Remove to a casserole.
2. Saute onion, shallots and parsley until limp. Sprinkle flour over mixture and stir well. Add wine and continue cooking until sauce has thickened.
3. Add sauce to casserole, cover loosely with foil, and bake in a 350° oven for 20 minutes. Remove cover and continue baking an additional 15 minutes.

Beer or apple juice may be substituted for the white wine. Omit the onion.

lamb and apple casserole

8 shoulder lamb chops
2 lbs. potatoes
4 T cooking oil
1 onion, chopped
3 apples, chopped
1 t brown sugar
½ t salt
¼ t pepper
1 C chicken broth

1. Slice the potatoes very thin. Arrange half of the potatoes in the bottom of a well greased baking dish.

2. Lightly brown the chops in the cooking oil. Remove from skillet and arrange over the potatoes.

3. In the same cooking oil, saute the onions and apples until both are tender. Remove and place over the chops.

4. Sprinkle the sugar, salt and pepper over all.

5. Cover with remaining potatoes. Pour in chicken broth.

6. Bake in a 350° oven for 1 hour.

lamb chops pizzaiola

6 shoulder lamb chops
3 T cooking oil
1 lb. potatoes, sliced
1 onion, sliced
1 Italian pepper, sliced
½ t oregano
2 lb. can tomatoes, chopped
½ C dry white wine

1. Brown chops on both sides in cooking oil. Remove from pan.

2. Place potatoes in the bottom of the same pan. Place chops over potatoes.

3. Top with remaining ingredients.

4. Cover and simmer over low heat for 1 hour.

hawaiian lamb chops

8 shoulder lamb chops

2 8½ oz. cans crushed pineapple, drained

4 t brown sugar
   margarine

1. Broil chops for 7 minutes on each side.

2. Spread pineapple on top. Sprinkle brown sugar over the pineapple. Dot with margarine.

3. Continue broiling to desired state of doneness (about 5 minutes).

For those who like it sweet.

quick breaded lamb chops

6 shoulder lamb chops
   bread crumbs

1. Press bread crumbs into lamb chops.

2. Broil to desired state of doneness.

This silly looking recipe is one of the best ways to prepare broiled shoulder chops.

To add zest, season the bread crumbs with any of the following herbs, spices or seasonings: ginger, lemon peel, mint, garlic, oregano, rosemary, sage, tarragon or thyme.

broiled ginger lamb riblets

5 lbs. lamb riblets
⅓ C ginger root, minced
⅓ C olive oil
⅓ C lemon juice
¼ C onion, minced
1½ T honey
1 T coriander
1½ t garlic salt
1 t cumin
½ t pepper
⅛ t cayenne pepper

1. Combine all ingredients and marinate overnight.

2. Remove meat to a broiler pan and broil, basting often with marinade, until ribs are cooked and nicely glazed.

lamb shanks braised in red wine

6 lamb shanks
flour
garlic salt
pepper
½ t oregano
cooking oil
1½ C dry red wine
½ C water
1 carrot, chopped
1 stalk celery, chopped
2 onions, chopped
1 bay leaf
⅛ t thyme

1. Dredge the lamb in flour. Sprinkle with garlic salt, pepper and oregano.

2. Brown shanks in cooking oil.

3. Add wine, water, carrots, celery, onions, bay leaf and thyme.

4. Simmer, covered, for 1½ hours.

Stuffed Lamb Shanks *may be prepared from this recipe.*

*Remove the shanks from the pan and set aside to cool. Reserve cooking broth. When the shanks are cool enough to handle, gently ease out the bones. Stuff the shanks with **1 cup of cooked rice** which has been seasoned with **½ teaspoon thyme, ½ teaspoon sage, 1 tablespoon minced parsley** and **2 minced shallots**. Arrange stuffed shanks in a baking dish; add the broth. Bake in a 350° oven for 20 minutes.*

dillkött på lamm
swedish lamb

6 lamb shanks
pepper
cooking oil
1 onion, chopped, sauteed
1½ C dry white wine
½ C beef broth
2 T flour mixed with 3 T water
1½ T dill
1 C non-dairy sour cream

1. Sprinkle shanks with pepper. Brown in cooking oil.

2. Place onions over shanks.

3. Add wine and broth. Cover and simmer 1½ hours. Remove meat to serving plate.

3. Strain cooking liquid. Add flour mixture and mix well. Cook over low heat until thickened. Remove from heat and stir in dill and non-dairy sour cream.

4. Pour over lamb and serve.

Dill is a common seasoning for lamb in the Swedish kitchen.

cranberry lamb

3 lbs. lamb for stewing (bone-in)
  cooking oil
1 onion, chopped
½ clove garlic, minced
6 oz. can tomato paste
1 C dry red wine
¼ t pepper
1½ C water
¾ C whole cranberry sauce
¼ t ginger
¼ t oregano

1. Brown lamb on all sides in cooking oil. Add onion, garlic, tomato paste, wine, pepper and water. Cover and simmer 30 minutes.

2. Add cranberry sauce, ginger and oregano. Continue to simmer an additional 30 minutes.

irish stew

2½ lbs. lamb for stewing (bone-in)
4 potatoes, sliced very thin
4 onions, sliced
¼ t thyme
1 t salt
1 t pepper
2 C water
4 potatoes, peeled and left whole

1. Place all ingredients, except whole potatoes, in a pot. Cover and simmer for 1½ hours.

2. Add the whole potatoes, cover and simmer an additional hour.

Real Irish stew contains no vegetables, except onions and potatoes, and no flour. The thinly sliced potatoes serve to thicken.

ragout d'agneau

3 lbs. lamb for stewing (bone-in)
  flour
1 clove garlic
1 t rosemary
¼ C cooking oil
1 t salt
½ t pepper
1 C dry white wine
1 C tomatoes, chopped
1 t tomato paste
¼ C water
1½ lbs. zucchini squash, cubed

1. Dredge lamb in flour.

2. Saute garlic and rosemary in cooking oil.

3. Add lamb and brown on all sides.

4. Add salt, pepper and wine. Add tomatoes, tomato paste and water. Simmer for 45 minutes.

5. Add squash and cook an additional 15 minutes.

morrocan lamb

3 lbs. lamb for stewing (bone-in)
½ C olive oil
¼ t ginger
½ t coriander
¼ t powdered saffron
3 onions, minced
1 clove garlic, minced
½ t salt
2 C water
2 lemons, quartered
24 small ripe olives

1. Combine all ingredients except lemons and olives. Bring to a boil, stirring occasionally. Add lemons and lower heat. Cover and simmer for 45 minutes.

2. Remove lamb and lemons to a warm plate. Reserve cooking liquid.

3. Boil cooking liquid 15 minutes.

4. Return lamb and lemons to sauce, lower heat. Add olives and heat through.

lamb stew

2 lbs. lamb for stewing (bone-in)
    cooking oil
½ t crushed red pepper
2 onions, chopped
4 potatoes, cubed
1 eggplant, cubed
3 green peppers, cut into strips
1½ C green beans, cut into 1″ pieces
1 C okra, cubed
4 tomatoes, sliced
3 eggs beaten
¼ C parsley, chopped

1. Brown meat on all sides in cooking oil. Remove to a casserole. Sprinkle with hot red pepper.

2. Saute each vegetable, except tomatoes, individually until tender. Layer over meat.

3. Add water to almost cover casserole ingredients. Bake in a 350° oven for 50 minutes.

4. Cover with tomatoes and cook an additional 10 minutes.

5. Combine eggs and parsley. Spoon over ingredients and continue to bake until egg mixture sets.

Commonly called **Ghivetch**, *this dish easily adapts to seasonal vegetables at hand.*

lamb and artichokes

3 lbs. lamb for stewing (bone-in)
  cooking oil
2 onions, chopped
2 stalks celery, diced
½ t salt
¼ t ground cumin
¼ t curry powder
¼ t pepper
⅛ t cinnamon
⅛ t allspice
8 oz. can tomato sauce
6 oz. can tomato paste
¾ C pineapple juice
2 t brown sugar
1 t soy sauce
1 t Worcestershire sauce
2 pkgs. frozen artichokes, thawed
  and drained

1. Brown lamb in cooking oil. Add onions and celery and continue cooking until onions are transparent.

2. Combine remaining ingredients, except artichokes, to make a sauce.

3. Arrange meat mixture and artichokes in a casserole. Pour sauce over all. Bake in a 325° oven for 1 hour.

braised lamb with avgolemono sauce

      3 lbs. lamb for stewing (bone-in)
         flour
      1 onion, minced
         cooking oil
      1 t salt
      ½ t pepper
      ¼ t marjoram
      ½ C dry white wine
      3 C vegetable broth
      3 egg yolks
      2 T lemon juice
      2 t parsley, minced

1. Dredge lamb in flour.

2. Saute onion in cooking oil until limp. Add salt, pepper and marjoram.

3. Add lamb and brown meat well on all sides.

4. Add wine and deglaze pan. Add vegetable broth and simmer 45 minutes.

5. Beat egg yolks, lemon juice and parsley together.

6. Add a small amount of sauce from the stew to the egg mixture. Then pour the tempered egg mixture into the stew, stirring constantly. Serve.

indian lamb curry

3 lbs. lamb for stewing (bone-in)
  cooking oil
1 onion, chopped
1 apple, chopped
½ t salt
¼ t pepper
1 t curry powder
½ t ginger
1 t sugar
2 C beef broth
5 T golden raisins
3 C cooked rice
  shredded, unsweetened coconut

1. Brown meat in cooking oil. Add remaining ingredients, except raisins, rice and coconut. Simmer, covered, for 1 hour.

2. Add raisins and cook an additional 15 minutes.

3. To serve: pour this mixture over hot rice and sprinkle with coconut.

Please note that the coconut is unsweetened and not the baking variety. It can usually be purchased in natural food stores.

alma mater lamb
lamb and peas

1½ lb. lean ground lamb
1 C bread crumbs
1 egg, slightly beaten
¼ C liquid non-dairy creamer
3 T catsup
¼ t salt
¼ t pepper
½ t rosemary
    cooking oil
2 onions, chopped, sauteed
1 C water
½ C red wine vinegar
2 T sugar
1 pkg. frozen peas, thawed, drained

1. Mix together the first 8 ingredients. Shape into small balls.

2. Brown balls thoroughly in cooking oil.

3. Add onions, water, vinegar and sugar. Cover and simmer for 30 minutes. Add peas and cook an additional 5 minutes.

My husband, a U. of P. alumnus, named this dish; he's quite a punster.

lazy baked kebbe

1 lb. lean ground lamb
⅓ C bulghur
   boiling water
1 onion, minced
4 oz. can tomato sauce
½ t salt
¼ t pepper
1 t cinnamon
¼ C pine nuts
3 T margarine, melted

1. Pour boiling water over bulghur and allow to stand for 30 minutes. Drain.

2. Combine bulghur, lamb, onion, tomato sauce, salt, pepper and cinnamon and mix well. Press into a greased baking dish.

3. Score diamond shaped slices into top. Press pine nuts onto the top.

4. Pour margarine over all.

5. Bake in a 400° oven for 30 minutes.

Great luncheon dish!

lamb stuffed eggplant

1 lb. lean ground lamb
3 eggplants
1 onion, minced
½ C uncooked rice
2 T fresh dill, chopped
2 T parsley, chopped
1 egg
3 T tomato paste
½ t pepper
1 C vegetable broth

1. Cut eggplant in half lengthwise. Scoop out and discard pulp.

2. Combine lamb, onion, rice, dill, parsley, egg, tomato paste and pepper.

3. Stuff eggplant lightly.

4. Place stuffed eggplant in skillet. Add vegetable broth and enough water to half cover eggplant.

5. Cook, covered, for 60 minutes.

This dish may be served either hot or cold.

lamb stuffed peppers

1 lb. lean ground lamb
½ C bulghur
boiling water
1 clove garlic, minced
⅓ C pine nuts
¼ C margarine
1 onion, minced
1 t mint
½ t thyme
½ t salt
½ t pepper
2 T Worcestershire sauce
¼ C dry white wine
4 bell peppers

1. Pour boiling water over bulghur and allow to stand for 30 minutes. Drain.

2. Saute the pine nuts and garlic in the margarine until golden.

3. Add the lamb, bulghur, onions, Worcestershire sauce and seasonings. Continue cooking until the lamb is well browned.

4. Add the wine and mix well. Reduce heat and keep warm.

5. Cut tops off peppers; scoop out the seeds. Par-boil and drain.

6. Spoon the lamb mixture into the prepared peppers.

lamb stuffed zucchini

1½ lbs. lean ground lamb
 6 zucchini squash
 1 onion, chopped
 2 cloves garlic, chopped
 2 T olive oil
 ¼ C uncooked rice
 2 t grated lemon peel
 ¼ t salt
 ½ t pepper
 2 t mint
 1 C chicken broth
 3 eggs
 1 T cornstarch
 ½ C lemon juice

1. Cut zucchini in half lengthwise. Scoop out centers and reserve pulp.

2. Saute onion and garlic in olive oil until translucent. Add lamb and cook until pink disappears.

3. Add rice, lemon peel, mint, reserved pulp, salt and pepper to the mixture. Cover and simmer 15 minutes.

4. Place zucchini shells in a baking dish. Fill with cooked lamb mixture. Pour chicken broth around the shells. Cover tightly and bake in a 375° oven for 25 minutes.

5. To make sauce, pour off stock and reduce to 1 cup.

6. Beat eggs and cornstarch together. Slowly beat in the lemon juice and the stock. Cook, stirring constantly, until sauce is thickened. Pour over stuffed zucchini shells and serve.

coq au vin

4 lb. chicken, pullet or roaster, cut
   into 10 pieces
  cooking oil
1 onion, minced
2 cloves garlic, minced
3 T flour
2 C dry red wine
2 C beef broth
4 shallots, minced
  bouquet garni:
   1 celery stalk
   3 sprigs parsley
   1 bay leaf
   ½ t thyme
1 T tomato paste
½ t salt
½ t pepper
½ lb. mushroom caps
16 small white onions
1 T margarine
1 T sugar

1. Brown chicken in cooking oil. Add onion and garlic and saute until golden. Sprinkle with flour and cook 3 minutes.

2. Pour in wine and beef broth. Add shallots, bouquet garni, tomato paste, salt and pepper. Stir well; cover and simmer 1½ hours.

3. Saute mushrooms in cooking oil. Set aside.

4. Braise onions in water for 10 minutes. Drain.

5. In fry pan, melt 1 tablespoon margarine. Add 1 tablespoon sugar and stir until dissolved. Add the onions and mushrooms and toss to glaze.

6. To serve: arrange chicken in center of platter and surround with mushrooms and onions.

white on white chicken

8 chicken cutlets
6 slices fresh white bread
  flour
2 eggs
¼ C water
¼ C liquid non-dairy creamer
½ t salt
½ t white pepper
  cooking oil
1 recipe Soubise Sauce

1. Coarsely chop bread in blender or food processor.

2. Pound chicken cutlets between 2 pieces of waxed paper to flatten slightly. Dust lightly with flour.

3. Beat eggs with water, liquid non-dairy creamer, salt and pepper.

4. Dip cutlets into egg mixture and then press into prepared crumbs.

5. Stack cutlets between layers of waxed paper. Refrigerate 3 hours or longer.

6. Fry quickly, on both sides, in a thin film of oil, until golden brown. Drain on paper towels and serve with **Soubise Sauce.**

The breast when cut in half and boned yields two cutlets.

soubise sauce

          2 onions, chopped
          6 mushrooms, sliced
          3 T margarine
          1 C cooked rice
        1¼ C chicken broth
          1 egg yolk
         ¼ C liquid non-dairy creamer
          2 T parsley, chopped
         ½ t salt
         ¼ t pepper
         ¼ t nutmeg

1. Saute onion and mushrooms in margarine until limp.
2. Add rice and chicken broth and simmer for 5 minutes.
3. In blender or food processor, combine onion mixture with ingredients and blend until smooth.

supreme de volaille chaud-froid

8 chicken cutlets
1 T lemon juice
¼ C dry white wine
¼ t salt
¼ t white pepper
14 T unsalted margarine, softened
½ C onions, minced
2 T shallots, minced
1 apple, chopped
1 lb. chicken livers, broiled
2 T apple juice
1 T liquid non-dairy creamer
1 t lemon juice
½ t salt
¼ t pepper
1 recipe Chaud-Froid Sauce, made with chicken stock

1. Place chicken in a large baking dish in a single layer, uncrowded. Combine lemon juice, wine, salt and pepper. Pour over chicken; cover and bake in a 350° oven for 20 minutes.

2. Remove chicken and cool. Slice in half horizontally; set aside.

3. Saute onions, shallots and apple in 3 tablespoons margarine. Set aside.

4. Puree chicken livers, 3 tablespoons margarine, apple juice and liquid non-dairy creamer in blender or food processor. Add apple mixture and blend until very smooth. Cool.

5. Combine liver mixture with 8 tablespoons margarine, lemon juice, salt and pepper. Blend thoroughly until smooth.

6. Place bottom half of chicken cutlets on wire rack. Spread with some chicken liver mixture. Place top half of chicken cutlets on top of liver. (Check to be sure all cutlets are filled.)

7. Coat chicken with **Chaud-Froid Sauce.** Recoat once.

8. Decorate as desired. Place on serving platter and chill. Serve cold.

Pour madame, we suggest flower blossoms made of green stuffed olives, black olives and scalloped carrots, all sliced thin. Blanch scallion stalks and cut into thin strips for stems. Using the same ingredients, create geometric patterns for the men.

chaud-froid sauce

¼ C stock (chicken, meat or fish)
1½ T white wine
1 T tarragon vinegar
2 t unflavored gelatin
2 C mayonnaise

1. Combine stock, wine and vinegar in top of double boiler.

2. Sprinkle gelatin over and allow to soften 5 minutes.

3. Heat over hot water until mixture is clear. Cool to room temperature.

4. Beat mayonnaise into mixture.

Use this mixture just before it sets to coat chicken, eggs, fresh vegetables, etc. This sauce is also used to bind salad mixtures which are to be molded.

calcutta cutlets

8 chicken cutlets
5 cloves garlic
2 slices ginger root
1 onion, quartered
4 canned hot green chili peppers
4 t ground cumin
4 t coriander leaves, chopped
6 T lime juice
¾ t salt
½ t pepper
2 eggs mixed with 2 T cold water
   bread crumbs
   cooking oil
   lime wedges

1. Combine garlic, ginger, onion, chili peppers, cumin, coriander, lime juice, salt and pepper in blender. Add 1 tablespoon water and blend until smooth to make a marinade.

2. Place marinade in a bowl with the chicken cutlets. Cover and refrigerate overnight.

3. Allowing marinade to cling to cutlets, dip cutlets into egg mixture and then into bread crumbs; coat thoroughly.

4. Fry cutlets in cooking oil until golden brown on both sides, about 15 minutes.

5. Garnish with lime wedges.

Coriander can usually be found in a Spanish or Portugese market as cilantro; or it may also be found in an oriental market as Chinese parsley.

chicken in curry sauce

8 chicken cutlets

3 C chicken broth

2 T margarine

2 T flour

1 C liquid non-dairy creamer

1 C mayonnaise

2 t curry powder

1. Poach chicken cutlets in broth until tender. Remove chicken and set aside. Reserve broth.

2. Melt margarine; stir in flour and cook 2 minutes, stirring constantly. Gradually add 2 cups of the reserved broth and cook until thickened. Add non-dairy creamer and mayonnaise. Add curry powder and continue to cook until heated through.

3. Arrange cutlets in a baking dish. Pour sauce over cutlets and bake in a 300° oven for 20 minutes.

chicken kiev

8 **chicken cutlets**
½ **lb. margarine**
  herb combinations: (choose one)
    chive, thyme, marjoram
    parsley, chive, shallots
    scallion, parsley, garlic
    garlic and tarragon
¼ **t salt**
¼ **t pepper**
  flour
2 **eggs mixed with 2 T cold water**
  bread crumbs
  cooking oil

1. Pound chicken cutlets thin between 2 sheets of waxed paper.

2. Cream margarine with the herb combination of one's choice. Divide into 8 portions and roll into 8 fingers. Freeze.

3. Sprinkle chicken cutlets with salt and pepper. Place one margarine finger on each cutlet. Roll securely to encase margarine; secure with tooth picks. Cover and refrigerate 3 hours.

4. Remove tooth picks. Dip chicken rolls in flour, egg mixture and bread crumbs. Chill thoroughly.

5. Deep-fry in cooking oil just before serving.

This is a difficult dish to prepare correctly. The margarine must be completely encased so that it does not run out while cooking. All preparation may be done ahead of time. However, the frying must be done just before serving.

Caution your guests: margarine may spurt out with the first cut.

chicken veronique

3½ lb. chicken, fryer or broiler, cut
     into 10 pieces
     flour, mixed with salt and pepper
     cooking oil
½ C chicken broth
½ C dry white wine
1 t Fines Herbes
1 bay leaf
1 egg yolk
1 T liquid non-dairy creamer
2 C seedless grapes

1. Lightly flour chicken pieces. Brown in cooking oil.

2. Add chicken broth, wine, and seasonings. Cover and simmer 40 minutes. Remove from heat.

3. Combine egg yolk, and non-dairy creamer; add to chicken. Add grapes. Return to heat and bring to serving temperature.

fines herbes

chives
cheveril
tarragon
basil

Mix herbs together in any combination.

Use all fresh herbs or all dried herbs; do not mix fresh and dried herbs together.

chicken marengo

2 2½ lb. chickens, fryer or broiler,
each cut into 10 pieces
flour mixed with salt and pepper
cooking oil
1 onion, chopped
1 clove garlic, minced
2 shallots, minced
2 t thyme
1 bay leaf
½ C dry white wine
½ C tomatoes, chopped
8 oz. mushrooms, sliced
2 oz. brandy
2 t parsley, chopped

1. Dredge chicken in flour mixture; brown in cooking oil.

2. Combine all ingredients, cover, and simmer 45 minutes or until chicken is tender.

This dish was created for Napoleon. Supposedly, it was served to him the evening before his victorious battle at Marengo in 1800.

chicken paprikash

2 2½ lb. chickens, fryer or broiler,
each cut into 10 pieces
cooking oil
2 scallions, minced
2 red onions, minced
2 T paprika
½ C dry white wine
½ t salt
2 C chicken broth
½ C non-dairy sour cream

1. Brown chicken in cooking oil. Remove chicken to a warm platter.

2. Add scallions and onions to cooking oil and saute until limp.

3. Stir in paprika and cook 2 minutes.

4. Return chicken to the pan, add wine, salt and enough chicken broth to barely cover. Cook, covered, about 30 minutes, or until the chicken is tender.

5. Stir non-dairy sour cream into chicken sauce. Cook until heated through.

One of the most famous of all Hungarian dishes, this should be made with the best quality paprika available.

chicken maryland

3 lb. frying chicken, cut into 10 pieces
   flour mixed with salt and pepper
1 egg mixed with 2 T water
1 C bread crumbs
   cooking oil
1 recipe Corn Fritters

1. Dredge chicken in flour.
2. Dip into egg mixture and then into crumbs.
3. Fry in 2 inches of cooking oil until golden on all sides.
4. Serve with **Corn Fritters.**

corn fritters

2 C whole kernel corn
1 C liquid non-dairy creamer
4 eggs, slightly beaten
1⅓ C flour
½ t salt
1 t baking powder
   cooking oil

1. Combine corn, non-dairy creamer and eggs.
2. Add flour, salt and baking powder. Beat until smooth.
3. Drop by tablespoons into 375° cooking oil to deep-fry. Drain and serve.

chicken cacciatora

3 lb. chicken, fryer or broiler, cut into
   10 pieces
   olive oil
1 clove garlic
2 t rosemary
½ t oregano
1 t salt
¼ C lemon juice
½ C dry white wine

1. Saute garlic in cooking oil. Discard garlic.

2. Brown chicken in this oil; sprinkle with rosemary, oregano and salt while cooking.

3. Add lemon juice and wine. Bring to a boil, reduce heat and simmer 20 minutes. Remove chicken to serving platter.

4. Add 1 tablespoon water to pan and deglaze. Pour sauce over chicken and serve.

One of the most famous of Italian chicken dishes, this recipe is from the northern region.

sicilian chicken cacciatora

3 lb. chicken, fryer or broiler, cut into
   10 pieces
   flour mixed with salt and pepper
   cooking oil
1 clove garlic, minced
1 C canned tomatoes
1 onion, sliced
1 carrot, chopped
1 stalk celery, chopped
1 T parsley, chopped
½ C dry white wine
1 C mushrooms, sliced

1. Dredge chicken in flour. Brown chicken in cooking oil.

2. Add garlic, tomatoes, onion, carrot, celery and parsley and simmer 40 minutes.

3. Add wine and mushrooms and simmer an additional 15 minutes.

arroz con pollo

3 lb. chicken, fryer or broiler, cut into
    10 pieces
    flour mixed with salt and pepper
4 shallots, minced
1 onion, sliced
4 oz. mushrooms, sliced
    cooking oil
3 tomatoes, quartered
2 C chicken broth
1 bay leaf
2 T parsley, minced
½ t saffron, soaked in 1 T boiling water
1 C rice, uncooked
2 green peppers, chopped
1 C sherry
½ C peas, cooked
6 asparagus tips, cooked
1 pimento, chopped

1. Saute shallots, onion and mushrooms in cooking oil until limp. Set aside.

2. Dredge chicken in flour mixture and brown in cooking oil.

3. Add mushroom mixture, tomatoes, chicken broth, bay leaf, and parsley. Cover and simmer 30 minutes.

4. Add saffron and rice and continue to cook, covered, for 20 minutes.

5. Add peppers and sherry and continue to cook 10 minutes.

6. To serve, garnish with peas, asparagus, and pimento.

This dish may also be cooked in the oven. After step 2, combine all ingredients except garnish. Place in a casserole and cook in a 350° oven, covered, for 45 minutes. Garnish and serve.

pollo fritto
fried chicken

> 3 lb. chicken, fryer or broiler, cut into
> 10 pieces
> ¼ C olive oil
> 2 T lemon juice
> 2 T parsley, chopped
> 1 t salt
> ½ t pepper
> flour
> 2 eggs, beaten
> cooking oil

1. Combine olive oil, lemon juice, parsley, salt and pepper.

2. Marinate chicken in this mixture for 2 hours. Drain and pat dry.

3. Dredge the chicken in flour. Dip thoroughly in beaten eggs.

4. Fry slowly in cooking oil until golden brown, about 15 minutes on each side.

5. Drain on paper towels and serve.

chicken with vermouth

> 3 lb. chicken, fryer or broiler, cut into
> 10 pieces
> 8 oz. can tomato sauce
> 1 T oregano
> ¼ C sweet vermouth
> ½ t garlic salt
> ½ t pepper

1. Brown chicken in a 500° oven for 30 minutes.

2. Place chicken and remaining ingredients in a saucepan and simmer 20 minutes.

3. Serve chicken with its sauce.

chicken tetrazzini

   3 C cooked white meat of chicken, diced
   5 T margarine
   3 T flour
1½ C chicken broth
   1 C liquid non-dairy creamer
   ½ C sherry
   ½ t salt
   ¼ t white pepper
   ¼ t nutmeg
   ½ lb. mushrooms, sliced, sauteed
   ½ lb. spaghetti, cooked
   ¼ C bread crumbs

1. Melt 3 tablespoons margarine; stir in flour and cook 2 minutes stirring constantly. Gradually add chicken broth, non-dairy creamer, sherry, salt, pepper and nutmeg. Cook, stirring, until thickened.

2. To half of this sauce, add the mushrooms and spaghetti. Pour into a greased baking dish. Make a hole in the center.

3. To the other half of the sauce, add the chicken. Pour into the center of the casserole.

4. Mix bread crumbs with 2 tablespoons melted margarine. Sprinkle over casserole.

5. Bake in a 400° oven for 25 minutes, or until heated through and browned.

This dish was created and named for the famous opera singer, Luisa Tetrazzini.

connecticut curried chicken

4 C cooked white meat of chicken,
   diced
2 oz. chicken fat
2 onions, sliced
1 carrot, sliced
2 celery stalks, sliced
1 apple, sliced
4 T curry powder
4 T flour
1 t tomato paste
2½ C chicken broth
1 T lemon juice
1 T honey
1 slice ginger root
4 cardamon seeds, crushed
1 clove garlic, crushed
½ t dry mustard
3 C cooked rice
4 Condiments

1. Saute onions, carrot, celery and apple in hot chicken fat for 5 minutes.

2. Add curry powder and cook 5 minutes.

3. Add flour and cook an additional 5 minutes. Remove from heat and add tomato paste, broth, lemon juice, honey, ginger, cardamon seeds, garlic and mustard.

4. Return to heat, bring to a boil and simmer 1 hour.

5. Remove ginger root and cardamon seeds.

6. Puree sauce in blender and pour over chicken.

7. Refrigerate overnight.

8. Reheat and serve with rice and any four **Condiments.**

condiments

chutney
toasted coconut flakes
currants
chopped green pepper
guava jelly
chopped, salted nuts
crushed, drained pineapple
raisins
chopped, hard cooked egg whites
sieved, hard cooked egg yolks

chicken a la king

3 C cooked white meat of chicken, diced
½ lb. mushrooms, sliced
10 T margarine
½ onion, minced
¾ C pimento, chopped
9 T flour
½ t salt
½ t white pepper
3 C chicken broth
1 C liquid non-dairy creamer
¼ t nutmeg
3 egg yolks
6 T sherry
6 Toast Cups

1. Saute mushrooms in 4 tablespoons margarine for 3 minutes. Add onion and pimento and saute an additional 3 minutes. Set aside.

2. Melt 6 tablespoons margarine; stir in flour, salt and pepper, and cook 2 minutes, stirring constantly. Gradually add the chicken broth, non-dairy creamer and nutmeg. Continue to cook, stirring, until thickened.

3. Combine mushroom mixture, the sauce and chicken. Heat through. Stir in egg yolks and sherry. Pour into **Toast Cups** and serve.

toast cups

Cut the crusts from **6 slices of fresh bread.** Fit into 6 muffin cups. Bake in a 350° oven until golden brown.

chicken souffle

2 C cooked chicken, ground
2 recipes Thick White Sauce
2 T onion, minced
1 T parsley, minced
3 egg yolks, slightly beaten
⅛ t white pepper
3 egg whites, beaten stiff
6 tart shells, unbaked

1. Combine chicken, white sauce, onion, parsley, egg yolks, and pepper.

2. Fold in egg whites.

3. Pour into tart shells. Place on cookie sheet and bake in a 400° oven for 25 minutes. Serve immediately.

california chicken salad

2 C cooked white meat of chicken, diced
1 avocado, cubed
1 C canned pineapple chunks, drained
½ C walnuts, chopped
2 T onion, minced
¼ t white pepper
½ C mayonnaise

Toss all ingredients together. Serve chilled, on a bed of lettuce.

This salad readily becomes the filling for a tea sandwich. Mince the first 5 ingredients rather fine; add the pepper and mayonnaise, mixing well. Spread on thinly sliced **Date Nut Bread**.

date nut bread

½ lb. dates, pitted, cut into thirds
1½ C boiling water
2 t baking soda
1½ C sugar
1 T margarine
1 egg
2¾ C flour, unsifted
½ t salt
1 t vanilla
½ lb. walnuts, coarsely chopped

1. Place dates in bowl. Pour boiling water over dates and set aside to cool. When tepid, add baking soda.

2. Cream sugar and margarine together. Add egg.

3. Alternately beat in flour and liquid from dates. Add salt and vanilla.

4. Fold in dates and nuts.

5. Lightly grease the bottom of a 5½ x 9½ x 3″ loaf pan. Pour in batter.

6. Bake on the center shelf of a 300° oven for 2 hours.

7. Remove from pan and turn on side to cool. Slice very thinly.

Do not use chopped dates but, rather, buy whole dates and cut as directed.

chicken in the round

3 C cooked chicken, ground
2 recipes Thick White Sauce
¼ lb. smoked dark meat turkey, ground
½ onion, minced
2 egg yolks, beaten
2 C bread crumbs
   cooking oil

1. Combine chicken, white sauce, ground turkey, onion and egg yolks. Mix well.

2. Shape into patties. Press into bread crumbs.

3. Fry quickly in cooking oil until golden brown.

chicken loaf

3 C cooked chicken, ground
1 C bread crumbs
2 T parsley, minced
3 T onion, minced
1 T celery salt
1 t thyme
1 green pepper, chopped
3 eggs, beaten

1. Combine all ingredients. Pack into a greased loaf pan.

2. Bake in a 350° oven for 1 hour.

monte cristo sandwich

- 3 T tehina
- 3 T tofu
- 18 thin slices challah, trimmed
  margarine, softened
- 6 slices smoked dark meat turkey
- 6 slices cooked white meat of
  chicken
- 2 eggs mixed with 2 t water
  margarine

1. Mash tehina and tofu together.
2. Layer as follows to make 6 sandwiches:
   1 slice of bread spread with softened
     margarine
   1 slice smoked turkey
   1 slice chicken
   1 slice of bread spread with softened
     margarine on both sides
   1 tablespoon tofu mixture
   1 slice of bread spread with softened
     margarine (margarine side down)
3. Dip each sandwich into the egg mixture.
4. Fry in margarine on all sides until golden
   brown.

Serve the sandwiches with a variety of jellies, jams, chutneys or cranberry sauce. Have guests choose their own.

eggs benedict

4 English muffins, split in half, toasted
8 thick slices smoked dark meat
   turkey
8 poached eggs
1 recipe Hollandaise Sauce
   parsley

1. Place one English muffin half on an individual plate; cover with a slice of smoked turkey.

2. Gently slip a poached egg on top of the turkey.

3. Mask the egg with **Hollandaise Sauce.** Garnish with a sprig of parsley.

4. Repeat until all are assembled.

hollandaise sauce

½ lb. margarine
4 egg yolks
2 T lemon juice
   pinch of salt
½ t dry mustard

1. Melt margarine to just below the boiling point.

2. Place all ingredients, except margarine, in blender. Blend 30 seconds.

3. With blender on, pour in melted margarine in a slow, steady stream.

If the sauce is heated to over 140°, (and less than 180°), it will separate around the edges of the pan. Add briskly, with a wire whisk, 1 or 2 tablespoons warm water to reconstitute. If the sauce is heated to over 180°, it will curdle. It is then, for most purposes, finished.

omelette

2 eggs
1 t water
  pepper (optional)
1 T margarine
  filling of one's choice

1. Add water and pepper to eggs, beating until just blended.

2. Melt the margarine over high heat, in an eight inch skillet with sloping sides. Swirl the margarine around the pan.

3. Pour all of the egg mixture into the pan and continue to swirl. Hold a fork horizontally above the egg mixture and with the flat sides of the tines, gently touch the egg mixture in the center of the pan, raising and lowering fork, as you continue to rotate pan.

4. As under section becomes set, lift it slightly and allow uncooked portion to flow underneath and cook. (Do not overcook the eggs; the omelette continues to cook after it has left the pan.)

5. Place the pan with the handle facing directly to the left. Visually divide the pan in half, left and right. Place desired filling over right hand side of cooked egg mixture.

6. With the handle still facing directly to the left, extend your left hand, palm side up, and grasp the handle. In right hand, hold serving plate against pan. Lift handle of pan towards plate. Omelette will roll over onto itself and then fall onto plate. Serve one; make another.

Use **Chicken Filling, Fines Herbes** *mixed with 1 tablespoon melted margarine, vegetables in any combination — i.e. a filling of one's choice.*

The step described in #3, builds up layers of egg, and produces a light, fluffy dish.

aspic

hard cooked eggs
cooked meat
cooked chicken
cooked vegetables
2 T unflavored gelatin
3 C broth, beef or chicken, all fat
    removed
1 t lemon juice
1 T sherry
½ t brandy
1 t tomato paste
2 sprigs parsley
½ C carrots, diced
½ C onions, diced
½ C celery, diced
¼ t thyme
1 clove

1. Sprinkle gelatin over ½ cup of broth. Allow to stand for 3 minutes. Heat over low heat until dissolved.

2. Add remaining broth, lemon juice, sherry, brandy, tomato paste, parsley, carrot, onion, celery and seasonings. Simmer 30 minutes.

3. Strain and cool.

4. Assemble as you would any gelatin mold, using eggs, meat, chicken and vegetables in any combination to suit one's taste.

Clear aspic, chopped, makes an excellent garnish.

SIDE DISHES

spinach salad omar

1 egg, beaten lightly
1 t sugar
½ t salt
¼ t dry mustard
¼ t paprika
½ t Worcestershire sauce
1 T catsup
½ C salad oil
⅛ C vinegar
1 lb. spinach, stems removed
1 hard cooked egg, minced

1. Combine first seven ingredients.
2. Stir into a smooth paste.
3. Alternately beat in oil and vinegar until dressing is smooth and thick.
4. Three hours before serving, pour the dressing over the spinach and toss well. Refrigerate until ready to serve.
5. Garnish with minced egg.

If this salad is prepared ahead of time, as suggested, the spinach will wilt and shrink considerably, but the flavor will be measurably enhanced.

hot spinach salad

1 lb. spinach, torn into bite size pieces
4 T imitation-bacon flavored bits
1 purple onion, chopped
  coarsely ground black pepper
3 T oil
2 T vinegar
1 t sugar

1. Place spinach in salad bowl.
2. Sprinkle imitation-bacon flavored bits, onion and black pepper over spinach.
3. Heat oil, vinegar and sugar together. Pour this dressing on spinach just before serving.

Washed salad greens should be thoroughly dried; this will allow the salad dressing to adhere to the leaf. Place the wet leaves in an impeccably clean pillow case; close and knot securely. Advance the cycle on your washing machine to spin-dry. Yes! The machine will do the work for you. Remove from machine and refrigerate greens in damp case until ready for use.

summer salad

3 garden fresh tomatoes
3 T olive oil
2 sprigs fresh basil, chopped
3 sprigs fresh parsley, chopped
1 red onion, sliced
½ t oregano
½ t salt

1. Cut tomatoes into bite size pieces.

2. Combine all ingredients and toss.

3. Allow to stand at room temperature for 30 minutes. Drain before serving.

fall salad

2 heads fennel
½ lb. mushrooms, sliced
½ t salt
¼ t pepper
⅛ t garlic powder
3 T olive oil
2 T red wine vinegar

1. Cut off the tops and hard outside stalks of the fennel. Cut into thin crosswise slices.

2. In a salad bowl toss fennel, mushrooms, salt, pepper, garlic powder and oil.

3. Sprinkle vinegar over all and toss again. Serve immediately.

Fennel is a seasonal Italian vegetable. It has an anise-like flavor. It's quite often eaten as one would eat a stalk of celery.

spring salad

1 head bibb lettuce
1 purple onion, sliced into rings
¼ lb. mushrooms, sliced thin
     violets
1 recipe French Dressing

1. Line a salad bowl with the lettuce.

2. In the center, place onion rings and mushrooms.

3. Sprinkle with violets. Serve with **French Dressing.**

In summer, substitute nasturtiums for violets.

french dressing

½ C olive oil
¼ C red wine vinegar
 1 t salt
¼ t ground black pepper
¼ t oregano

Combine all ingredients well.

peacock salad

1 lb. Belgian endives
2 pink grapefruits, sectioned
1 recipe Mustard Dressing

1. Gently break the endives into leaves and arrange in a fan shape on individual salad plates.
2. Arrange the grapefruit sections at the bottom of the fan.
3. Just before serving, spoon on **Mustard Dressing.**

Short on grapefruit? Serve just endives with **Honey Dressing**. *Or, if you have fruit for a salad, use* **Celery Seed Dressing**, *and serve the salad with* **Date Nut Bread**.

mustard dressing

3   shallots
2   cloves garlic
1½ t salt
½   t pepper
1   T Dijon-style mustard
⅓   C vinegar
1   T sugar
⅔   C oil

Place all ingredients, except oil, in the blender for 1 minute. Add the oil and blend until smooth.

honey dressing

⅔ C sugar
1 t dry mustard
1 t paprika
¼ t salt
1 t celery seed
⅓ C honey
5 T vinegar
1 T lemon juice
1 t onion, grated
1 C olive oil

1. Mix dry ingredients together.
2. Add honey, vinegar, lemon juice and onion.
3. Beat oil into mixture slowly.

Serve over endives, chicory, rugula, or any bitter tasting green.

celery seed dressing

1 C sugar
1½ t flour
¼ t dry mustard
1 T paprika
½ C vinegar
2½ t onion juice
1 C olive oil
1 T celery seed

1. Mix together sugar, flour, mustard and paprika.
2. Add vinegar and cook 2 minutes. Cool.
3. Stir in onion juice.
4. Beat oil in slowly.
5. Add celery seed. Stir well.

Use prepared onion juice, or scrape a raw onion to create your own.

carrot salad

½ C vinegar
¾ C sugar
1 t Worcestershire sauce
1 t dry mustard
½ C oil
10 oz. can tomato soup
1 lb. 10 oz. bag frozen, sliced carrots, thawed
1 onion, sliced thin
1 green pepper, sliced thin

1. Combine vinegar and sugar and bring to a boil. Cool.
2. Add Worcestershire sauce and mustard.
3. Combine all ingredients and chill.

An ideal accompaniment to any corned beef dish.

lentil salad

1 C lentils
½ C dill pickles, chopped
¼ C scallions, sliced
3 T capers, chopped
4 T parsley, minced
3 T vinegar
5 T olive oil
½ t tarragon

1. Cover lentils with water and soak for 1 hour. Drain.
2. Generously cover lentils with water; bring to a boil. Cook for 10 minutes. Drain.
3. Combine all ingredients and chill.

Individual portions of this salad are attractively served in **Starburst Tomato Cups***. Cut a* **firm tomato** *into wedges, being careful not to slice all the way through. The dark lentil salad, when placed in the center of the red tomato, is appealing to the eye as well as the palate.*

polynesian salad

16 oz. can bean sprouts
 8 oz. can bamboo shoots
 8 oz. can water chestnuts
14 oz. can hearts of palm
 1 head romaine lettuce
 2 tomatoes, diced
½ lb. mushrooms, sliced
 1 recipe Nani Dressing

1. Chill the cans in the refrigerator overnight. Drain all cans of liquid before assembling.

2. Line a salad bowl with romaine lettuce.

3. Make a mound of tomatoes in the center of the bowl.

4. Rinse the bean sprouts in cold water; drain. Shred the bamboo shoots into match stick size pieces. Quarter the water chestnuts; shred the hearts of palm. Arrange in separate mounds around the tomatoes. Top with mushrooms.

5. Dribble **Nani Dressing** over all.

nani dressing

1 C mayonnaise
2 oz. soy sauce
2 T lemon juice

Combine all ingredients.

sicilian potato salad

6 potatoes, peeled, boiled, do not cool
3 T olive oil
2 T wine vinegar
1 t salt
½ t pepper

1. Cut potatoes into bite size pieces.
2. Toss with remaining ingredients and serve warm.

artichoke and rice salad

2 C cooked rice, cooled
2 scallions, sliced
1 green pepper, diced
8 green olives, halved
2 6 oz. jars marinated artichoke hearts
¼ t curry powder
⅓ C mayonnaise

1. Add scallions, pepper and olives to the rice.
2. Drain artichoke hearts and reserve marinade.
3. Add curry powder and mayonnaise to the marinade and mix until well blended. Add the rice mixture and mix well.
4. Toss in the artichoke hearts. Cover bowl and refrigerate until well chilled.

indian rice

1 C rice
2 carrots
3 T margarine
3 T golden raisins
2 T sugar
2½ C chicken broth
½ t salt
¼ t mace
¼ t nutmeg
¼ t cinnamon
¼ t ground cardamon

1. Cut carrots into julienne sticks. Saute in margarine for 10 minutes.

2. Add raisins, rice, and sugar and continue sauteeing until rice turns golden.

3. Add chicken broth and seasonings. Bring to a boil and simmer until rice is cooked and liquid is absorbed.

Add more broth if liquid is absorbed before rice is cooked.

hawaiian rice

1½ C rice
1 onion, sliced
2 T margarine
1 bay leaf
½ lb. spinach
¼ C dry white wine
4 C chicken broth
¼ t salt
¼ t white pepper
1 C shredded, unsweetened coconut

1. Saute onion in margarine until limp. Add rice and saute until golden.

2. Add bay leaf, spinach, and wine. Cook, stirring, until spinach is limp.

3. Add broth, salt and pepper. Bring to a boil and simmer until rice is cooked and liquid is absorbed.

4. Add coconut and cook an additional 5 minutes.

Please note that the coconut is unsweetened and not the baking variety. It can usually be purchased in natural food stores.

polenta

1½ C cornmeal
1½ C cold water
1 t salt
3 C boiling water
3 T margarine, melted

1. Mix cornmeal, cold water and salt together.

2. Gradually add cornmeal mixture to boiling water, stirring constantly.

3. Cook over low heat, stirring frequently, until mixture is thick, about 10 minutes.

4. Beat in margarine and serve.

Polenta has many names. In the South, it's called **Grits**, *in Roumania, it's called* **Mamaliga** *and in Italy,* **Polenta**.

nockerl

2 eggs
1 C flour
6 T margarine, melted
1 T liquid non-dairy creamer

1. Combine eggs, flour, 1 tablespoon margarine and liquid non-dairy creamer to make a soft dough.

2. Beat in an electric mixer for 2 minutes.

3. Bring 4 quarts of water to a rolling boil. Put dough through a spaetzle sieve and drop into boiling water. Boil 2 minutes.

4. Drain and rinse with cold water. Toss with remaining margarine. To reheat, add more melted margarine.

linguine al pesto

2 C fresh basil
½ C parsley
6 oz. pignoli (pine nuts)
1 clove garlic
1¼ C olive oil
½ lb. linguine

1. Place basil, parsley, pine nuts and garlic in blender. Slowly add olive oil, blending at medium speed.

2. Cook linguine and drain. Toss immediately with the pesto sauce.

On occasion, substitute walnuts for pignoli.

One-half ounce dried basil may be substituted for the fresh.

apple chutney

5 C apples, chopped
3 oz. candied ginger, chopped
1 clove garlic, minced
1½ C golden raisins
2¼ C brown sugar
1 lemon, seeded, chopped
2 C cider vinegar
1½ t salt
4 oz. mustard seed

1. Combine all ingredients and bring to a boil.

2. Reduce heat and simmer 45 minutes.

3. Refrigerate and serve cold.

cranberry chutney

1 lb. fresh cranberries
4 pears, diced
2 lbs. light brown sugar
4 C golden raisins
3 C cider vinegar
4 t salt
1 spice bag:
  8 cloves
  20 allspice
  2 T mixed pickling spices

1. Combine all ingredients and bring to a boil.

2. Reduce heat and simmer 1 hour.

3. Discard spice bag.

4. Refrigerate and serve cold.

melon chutney

    3 C melon meat underripe, sliced
         thin
    1 pt. cider vinegar
  1½ C light brown sugar
    1 spice bag:
         1 cinnamon stick
         2 cardamon seeds
        ½ t anise seed
        ½ t coriander seed
        ½ t mustard seed
    2 T salt
   ⅛ t cayenne pepper
   ⅛ t mace
    2 cloves garlic, minced
    2 canned hot green chilis, sliced
    2 C golden raisins
   ¼ lb. dried apricots, sliced
   ½ C candied ginger, chopped
    1 C water

1. Combine vinegar, sugar, spice bag, salt, cayenne, mace and garlic. Boil, uncovered, for 15 minutes.

2. Add remaining ingredients, except melon, and simmer, covered, for 30 minutes.

3. Add melon and simmer, uncovered, for 45 minutes. Discard spice bag.

4. Refrigerate and serve cold.

peach chutney

  1 lb. 13 oz. can sliced peaches
  ½ C syrup from peaches
  1 lemon, sliced thin
  ½ C green pepper, chopped
  2 T onion, chopped
  ½ C brown sugar
  ½ C cider vinegar
  3 T candied ginger, chopped
  ½ t salt
  ⅛ t cloves
  ⅛ t nutmeg
  ⅛ t cayenne pepper
  ¼ t black pepper

1. Combine all ingredients and bring to a boil.

2. Reduce heat and simmer for 2 hours.

3. Refrigerate and serve cold in peach halves, for visual effect.

pineapple chutney

  3½ C fresh pineapple, cubed
  3 C cider vinegar
  3 C light brown sugar
  1 C golden raisins
  1 C currants
  1 C dates, chopped
  ¼ C lemon juice
  3 T ginger root, minced
  1 t salt
  ½ t ground allspice
  2 T capers

1. Bring all ingredients to a boil.

2. Cook over high heat, stirring occasionally, for 45 minutes.

3. Refrigerate and serve cold.

pickled oranges

    6 juice oranges
    1 t salt
  2½ C sugar
   ½ C water
   ¼ C light corn syrup
   ½ C cider vinegar
   24 cloves
    6 cinnamon sticks

1. Prick oranges. Cover with water, add salt and boil for 20 minutes. Drain.

2. Add fresh boiling water and continue boiling 20 minutes more. Drain and cool enough to handle.

3. Cut into quarters, discarding seeds. Place in shallow baking dish.

4. Combine sugar, water, corn syrup and vinegar and boil until the sugar dissolves. Add cloves and cinnamon sticks and boil an additional 10 minutes.

5. Pour the syrup over the oranges and bake, covered, in a 275° oven for 1 hour and 30 minutes. Refrigerate and serve cold.

Do not substitute ground cinnamon for cinnamon stick.

sicilian orange salad

    3 oranges, seeded
    1 red onion, sliced
   ½ t oregano
    1 T water
    3 T olive oil
   ½ t salt
   ¼ t crushed red pepper

1. Peel oranges and cut into bite size pieces.

2. Combine oregano, water, oil, salt and crushed pepper.

3. Toss all ingredients together.

sesame asparagus

1 lb. asparagus, cut into 1″ pieces
1 T cooking oil
2 t soy sauce
1 T sesame seeds

1. Stir-fry asparagus in cooking oil for 3 minutes.
2. Add soy sauce and sesame seeds and stir-fry an additional minute.

Color, taste and texture are excellent.

spicy beets

1 lb. beets, sliced
¼ t cloves
1 t grated orange peel
3 T honey
¼ C dry red wine
2 T margarine

1. Cook beets and drain.
2. Combine remaining ingredients and bring to a boil.
3. Combine beets and sauce. Serve hot.

braised cabbage

1 onion, sliced
2 T margarine
3 C cabbage, shredded
3 carrots, shredded
½ t salt
¼ t oregano

1. Saute onion in margarine until limp.

2. Add cabbage, carrots and salt. Cover and cook for 5 minutes.

3. Remove cover and stir once quickly. Cover and cook an additional 5 minutes.

4. Remove from heat; then stir in oregano. Do not reheat.

Even the children like this one.

german red cabbage

1 red cabbage, shredded
2 T margarine
4 apples, chopped
1 onion, chopped
1 t sugar
¼ t cloves
   vinegar and water in equal amounts
1 C red wine

1. Melt margarine. Add cabbage, apples, onion, sugar, cloves and enough vinegar and water to cover ingredients.

2. Simmer, covered for 2 hours.

3. Add wine and continue cooking, uncovered, until liquid is absorbed.

carrot chutney

3 C carrots, chopped
2 C apples, chopped
½ C onion, chopped
½ C green pepper, chopped
1 orange, sliced thin
3 C cider vinegar
1 lb. dark brown sugar
1 t salt
1½ t cinnamon
½ t cloves
¼ t ginger
½ t hot sauce

1. Combine all ingredients and bring to a boil.
2. Reduce heat and simmer for 1 hour.
3. Refrigerate and serve cold.

ginger carrots

1 lb. carrots, sliced
2 T sugar
1½ t ginger
¼ C water
2 T margarine
¼ C light corn syrup

1. Cook carrots in water until tender. Drain and set aside.
2. Combine remaining ingredients and bring to a boil.
3. Combine carrots and sauce. Serve hot.

onions and prunes

1 lb. prunes, pitted
¾ C dry red wine
2 lb. small white onions
2 T margarine
2 T brown sugar

1. Soak prunes in wine for 4 hours; drain. Reserve marinade.

2. Melt margarine and sugar together. Add onions and cook until onions are lightly browned.

3. Add prunes and ¼ cup marinade. Cover and simmer until tender.

curried corn souffle

2 T margarine
2 T flour
½ t salt
¼ t white pepper
½ t caraway seeds
½ t curry powder
1 C liquid non-dairy creamer
17 oz. can whole kernel corn, drained
3 eggs, separated

1. Melt margarine; stir in flour and seasonings. Cook for 2 minutes, stirring constantly. Gradually add non-dairy creamer and cook until thick.

2. Add corn and mix well. Remove from heat.

3. Beat egg yolks until thick and lemon colored. Stir into corn mixture.

4. Beat egg whites stiff; fold into corn mixture.

5. Pour into a greased 2 quart casserole. Bake in a 325° oven for 45 minutes.

minted green beans

1 lb. green beans
1 clove garlic
3 T olive oil
2 T vinegar
⅛ t crushed red pepper
1 T mint

1. Cook green beans in boiling water until tender. Drain. Set aside.
2. Brown garlic in olive oil. Discard garlic.
3. Combine all ingredients and cook, uncovered, over low heat for 10 minutes.
4. Serve at room temperature.

green beans provencal

1 onion, sliced
  cooking oil
35 oz. can tomatoes
1½ lb. fresh green beans
2 T parsley, minced
1 t basil
½ t sugar
1 t salt
½ t pepper
½ t oregano

1. Saute onion in oil until limp.
2. Add remaining ingredients. Bring to a boil. Reduce heat, and simmer, uncovered, for 10 minutes, or until beans are tender.

hearty green bean casserole

4 hard cooked eggs
1 T onion, grated
2 T mayonnaise
2 pkgs. frozen French style green
    beans, thawed, drained
1 t savory
1 C mushrooms, sliced, sauteed
1½ recipes Thick White Sauce
2 oz. sherry
    bread crumbs
    margarine

1. Cut eggs in half. Gently remove yolks and mix with onion and mayonnaise. Stuff firmly into whites. Place in bottom of greased casserole.

2. Toss green beans with savory. Combine with mushrooms, **Thick White Sauce** and sherry. Pour over eggs.

3. Sprinkle with bread crumbs; dot with margarine.

4. Bake in a 350° oven for 40 minutes.

celery casserole

4 C celery, cut into 1'' pieces
2 T margarine
2 T flour
½ C chicken broth
½ C liquid non-dairy creamer
¼ C pimento, chopped
5 oz. can water chestnuts, drained, sliced
½ t salt
¼ t white pepper
½ C bread crumbs
2 T margarine, melted
¼ C almonds, sliced

1. Cook celery in boiling water for 4 minutes. Drain and set aside.

2. Melt margarine; stir in flour and cook for 2 minutes, stirring constantly. Gradually add chicken broth and non-dairy creamer and cook until thick.

3. Mix celery, pimento, water chestnuts, salt and pepper together. Add sauce and mix well.

4. Pour into a greased 1½ quart casserole.

5. Combine bread crumbs, melted margarine and almonds. Sprinkle over top.

6. Bake in a 350° oven for 30 minutes.

m-m-m mushrooms

12 large mushroom caps
 3 T olive oil
 1 T lemon juice
 ¼ t salt
 4 T margarine
 1 T chives, minced

1. Combine mushrooms, olive oil, lemon juice and salt. Marinate for 3 hours. Remove mushrooms and reserve marinade.

2. Brown mushrooms on both sides in 3 tablespoons margarine. Remove to serving platter.

3. In the same pan melt the remaining margarine; add reserved marinade and chives. Stir once and pour over mushrooms.

Do not overcook the chives; the distinctive flavor of this dish will be lost.

peas to please

2 pkg. frozen peas
¼ t rosemary
1 C water chestnuts, diced
¾ C canned mushrooms, sliced
3 T margarine
½ t salt
¼ t pepper

1. Cook peas with rosemary. Drain and set aside.

2. Saute water chestnuts and mushrooms in margarine for 3 minutes.

3. Combine peas, mushroom mixture, salt and pepper. Serve hot.

pommes de terre dauphine

1 C mashed potatoes
¼ t salt
½ C water
4 T margarine
½ C flour
2 eggs
1 C almonds, crushed
  cooking oil

1. Combine salt, water and margarine. Bring to a rolling boil. Add flour and cook, stirring, for 1 minute. Cool.

2. Beat in eggs one at a time.

3. Add mashed potatoes and mix well.

4. Shape into 30 balls; roll in nuts.

5. Deep-fry in 375° cooking oil, until golden.

french fried eggplant

3 lbs. eggplant
flour
2 eggs
½ C liquid non-dairy creamer
½ t salt
¼ t pepper
½ C matzo meal
½ t seasoned salt

1. Peel and cut eggplant into fingers. Dredge in flour.

2. Combine egg, non-dairy creamer, salt and pepper. Dip eggplant into this mixture.

3. Roll eggplant in matzo meal.

4. Deep-fry in 375° oil for 5 minutes.

5. Drain and sprinkle with seasoned salt. Serve immediately.

This is a great family dish, but cannot be prepared ahead of time for company. If reheated, the eggplant becomes limp.

green tomatoes

1¾ lbs. green tomatoes, sliced ¼″ thick
flour
2 t sugar
¼ t salt
⅛ t pepper
cooking oil

1. Dredge tomato slices in flour. Sprinkle with sugar, salt and pepper on both sides.

2. Saute tomatoes in cooking oil until lightly browned on both sides.

A great way to use end of the season, green tomatoes from your garden.

acorn squash boats

4 acorn squash
1 recipe Creamed Onions

1. Cut squash in half. Remove seeds.

2. Place in a baking dish, cut side up, and surround with 1 inch of hot water. Cover tightly with foil.

3. Cook in a 375° oven for 45 minutes.

4. To serve: spoon hot **Creamed Onions** into squash halves, or use a filling of your choice.

creamed onions

24 small white onions, boiled, drained
3 T margarine
3 T flour
½ t salt
⅛ t white pepper
½ t marjoram
½ t thyme
1½ C liquid non-dairy creamer

1. Melt margarine; stir in flour and cook 2 minutes, stirring constantly. Gradually add liquid non-dairy creamer and seasonings and cook until thick.

2. Mix onions and sauce together and heat through.

savory summer squash

3 lb. summer squash cut into 2″ fingers
2 T cooking oil
1 clove garlic, minced
3 T parsley, minced
2 T basil, minced
½ t salt
¼ t pepper

Heat cooking oil. Add all ingredients, cover and cook, stirring occasionally, until just tender. Do not overcook.

There are almost 20 varieties of summer squash. The cook may choose her own favorite for this recipe; ours is zucchini.

fried zucchini

2 lbs. zucchini squash, sliced
1 clove garlic
   cooking oil
3 T vinegar
1 t salt
⅛ t crushed red pepper

1. Brown garlic in cooking oil. Discard garlic.

2. In seasoned oil, fry zucchini on both sides until golden brown. Remove each piece from the pan as it becomes done. Drain on paper towels.

3. Drain oil from skillet. Return all squash to pan. Add salt, vinegar and pepper.

4. Simmer gently for 5 minutes. Remove to serving dish. Allow to cool slightly before serving.

roasted italian peppers

2 lb. Italian frying peppers, red or
     green
1 t salt
2 T olive oil

1. Wipe peppers with a damp towel.

2. Place on an outdoor grill and roast over hot coals until the skin is black and blistered and no uncharred portion remains. Turn peppers with tongs; do not pierce with fork.

3. When the skin is completely charred, remove to a brown paper bag. Close bag.

4. When cooled, remove the black skin. Cut off top stem and take out seeds. Tear peppers into strips. Sprinkle with salt and olive oil. Serve warm.

An indoor charcoal-type broiler, of course, serves well. A gas or an electric stove can be adapted by placing a wire rack over the burner. But, do not attempt this recipe in an electric oven.

Red **Roasted Italian Peppers** *may be sprinkled with lemon juice.*

Mix green **Roasted Italian Peppers** *with* **Italian Tomato Sauce I**. *Serve warm but not hot.*

DESSERTS

creme brulee

3 C liquid non-dairy creamer

6 egg yolks

2 T sugar

1 t vanilla

⅓ C brown sugar

fruits: sliced strawberries, sliced bananas, pineapple chunks, Mandarin orange sections

1. Heat non-dairy creamer until just below the boiling point.

2. In another saucepot, beat egg yolks and sugar with a wire whisk until well blended. Slowly stir in the heated non-dairy creamer. Cook, stirring constantly, until the mixture coats the back of a wooden spoon, about 15 minutes.

3. Stir in vanilla. Pour into a 1½ quart broiler-safe casserole. Refrigerate for 6 hours.

4. Sift brown sugar evenly over the top of the chilled casserole. Place under the broiler for 3 minutes, or until sugar is all melted.

5. Remove from oven and return to refrigerator. Chill until surface is hard.

6. To serve: place the casserole in the center of a large tray. Surround it with an assortment of fruit. With a serving spoon, tap the carmelized shell of the **Creme Brulee** and break it. Place a selection of fruit on an individual plate; spoon some of the **Creme Brulee** over the fruit.

"Brulee" means "burnt". However, just melt the sugar, do not burn it.

egg puff

½ C flour
½ C liquid non-dairy creamer
 2 eggs, lightly beaten
⅛ t nutmeg
 1 T lemon juice
 4 T margarine
 2 T confectioners sugar

1. Combine flour, non-dairy creamer, eggs, nutmeg and lemon juice. Beat lightly, leaving batter slightly lumpy.

2. Heat oven to 425°. Melt margarine in a 10 inch skillet in the oven. When very hot, pour in the batter.

3. Bake in a 425° oven for 20 minutes.

4. Remove from oven and sprinkle with confectioners sugar.

coffee blancmange

 1 t instant coffee
½ C water
15 marshmallows
½ t brandy
 1 C non-dairy whipping cream, whipped stiff

1. Combine coffee, water and marshmallows in top of double boiler; heat over water until marshmallows dissolve.

2. Cool and add brandy.

3. Fold whipped non-dairy creamer into coffee mixture and pour into 6 dessert glasses. Chill for several hours.

dessert crepes

  1   C less 2 T flour
  ⅛   t salt
  3   eggs
  2   T margarine, melted
1½   C stale beer
  2   T sugar

1. Combine all ingredients and process in blender.
2. Place in refrigerator for 2 hours. Blend again.
3. Cook crepes on both sides, over medium high heat, in a well greased crepe pan. Crepes should be lightly colored but not brown. Yields 20.

Crepes may be stacked between sheets of waxed paper and frozen.

crepes suzette

  8   T margarine
  ¼   C sugar
  1   T grated orange peel
  ⅓   C orange juice
  2   oz. orange flavored liqueur
  1   recipe Dessert Crepes
       confectioners sugar

1. Cream margarine and gradually add sugar. Beat in orange peel.
2. Beat in liquids, a few drops at a time.
3. Spread inside of each crepe with the sauce. Fold in quarters and arrange in a greased flame proof serving dish. Dot the crepes with the remaining sauce.
4. At serving time, heat crepes for 5 minutes in a 400° oven. Sprinkle with confectioners sugar and serve.

chocolate mousse

4 oz. sweet baking chocolate
4 eggs, separated
4 T unsalted margarine

1. Place chocolate in sauce pan and cover with hot tap water. When the point of a knife will penetrate the chocolate easily, pour off the water.

2. Add yolks to chocolate and whisk together.

3. Add margarine and place over low heat, stirring until margarine is melted. Remove to mixing bowl. Cool.

4. Beat egg whites until stiff. Fold into cooled chocolate mixture.

5. Place in glass bowl and refrigerate overnight.

pots de creme au chocolate

¾ C liquid non-dairy creamer
6 oz. chocolate chips
1 egg
½ t vanilla
1¾ T brandy
    pinch salt
2 T sugar

1. Heat the non-dairy creamer to the boiling point.

2. Place remaining ingredients in blender. Add the non-dairy creamer while blending.

3. Pour into 6 pots de creme cups and chill for 5 hours.

chocolate nut crunch

    2 C vanilla wafer crumbs
    1 C walnuts, chopped
    ½ C margarine
    1 C confectioners sugar
    3 egg yolks, well beaten
 1½ oz. unsweetened chocolate,
        melted
    ½ t vanilla
    3 egg whites, beaten stiff

1. Combine crumbs and nuts. Line bottom of 9 inch square pan with half of the crumbs.

2. Thoroughly cream margarine and sugar; add egg yolks. Add chocolate and vanilla. Mix well.

3. Fold in egg whites. Spread this mixture over crumbs. Top with remaining crumb mixture.

4. Refrigerate overnight.

5. To serve: cut into squares.

baked alaska

1 **pound cake 9x5x3″**
1 **recipe Non-Dairy Ice Cream**
6 **egg whites**
¾ **C sugar**
½ **t vanilla**
   dash of salt

1. Line a cookie sheet with a double layer of brown paper.

2. Slice the cake into 8 pieces. Place flat on brown paper.

3. Beat egg whites until they form soft peaks; gradually beat in sugar, vanilla and salt. Continue beating until stiff.

4. Slice ice cream into 8 pieces. Place 1 piece of ice cream on top of each slice of cake.

5. Generously cover each stack with meringue, taking care to completely seal cake and ice cream at all points.

6. Bake immediately in a 450° oven for 5 minutes, or until golden brown. Serve immediately.

This dessert is often served flaming. Carefully crack the eggs and reserve 8 well formed egg shell halves. Place the shells in the meringue before baking. After removing from the oven, fill shells with liqueur. Ignite and serve while flaming.

non-dairy ice cream

3 egg whites
6 T sugar
1 t vanilla
  dash of salt
4 drops red food coloring
5 oz. non-dairy whipping cream,
  whipped stiff

1. Beat egg whites until they form soft peaks; gradually beat in sugar, vanilla, salt and food coloring. Continue beating until stiff.

2. Fold in whipped non-dairy whipping cream.

3. Pour into an 8½ x 5″ loaf pan; freeze overnight.

biscuit tortoni

5 oz. non-dairy whipping cream,
  whipped stiff
¼ C almonds, toasted, chopped
¼ C shredded coconut, toasted
¾ t almond extract
1 egg white
2 T almonds, sliced

1. Mix together the non-dairy whipping cream, chopped almonds, coconut and almond extract.

2. Beat egg white until stiff; fold into nut mixture.

3. Spoon mixture into 8 foil or paper baking cups.

4. Sprinkle with sliced almonds.

5. Freeze overnight. Serve from freezer.

zabaglione

6 egg yolks
6 T sugar
¾ C sweet white wine

1. Mix egg yolks and sugar together. Add wine.

2. Place over boiling water and cook, beating constantly with a wire whisk, until foamy, then thick.

3. Remove from heat and pour into individual serving glasses. Repeat: do not allow bottom of pan to touch water.

Orange juice is also a suitable substitute for the Marsala wine classically used in this recipe.

pastine con i pignoli
pine nut cookies

8 oz. almond paste
2 egg whites
½ C sugar
½ C confectioners sugar
¼ C flour
⅛ t salt
3 oz. Italian pignolias (pine nuts)
   confectioners sugar

1. Mix almond paste and egg whites. Beat well until blended and smooth.

2. Stir in granulated and confectioners sugar, flour and salt.

3. Form dough into 1 inch balls and place on lightly greased cookie sheet 2 inches apart.

4. Press pine nuts into balls.

5. Bake in a 300° oven for 20 minutes.

6. Cool; sprinkle with confectioners sugar.

7. Store several days in a covered container to mellow. Makes 30 cookies.

baba au rhum

½ C margarine
½ C water
3½ C flour
¼ C sugar
¼ t salt
2 pkg. dry yeast
6 eggs
1 C currants
1 recipe Rum Sauce
⅓ C apricot jam
1 T lemon juice

1. Melt margarine in water. Set aside to cool to 130°.

2. Combine ¾ cup flour, sugar, salt and yeast.

3. In a mixer set on low speed, gradually pour margarine mixture into flour mixture. Beat at medium speed 2 minutes.

4. Beat in eggs and 1 cup flour and beat 2 minutes more.

5. With a spoon, stir in currants and enough flour to make a soft dough (about 1¾ cups flour).

6. Grease a 10 inch tube pan. Spread dough in pan. Cover and let rise until dough reaches the top of the pan.

7. Bake in a 375° oven for 40 minutes. Cool slightly in pan on a wire rack.

8. Prick baba with a fork and spoon on **Rum Sauce**. Let stand 2 hours to absorb sauce.

9. Press apricot jam through a sieve. Add lemon juice. Spoon over baba just before serving.

rum sauce

3 C water
2¼ C sugar
6 thin orange slices
6 thin lemon slices
1¼ C light rum

1. Bring water, sugar and fruit slices to a boil and simmer 5 minutes.

2. Cool sauce; discard fruit slices. Stir in rum.

walnut gateau

4 egg whites
1 t vanilla
1 t vinegar
1⅓ C sugar
1⅓ C walnuts, ground fine
2 C non-dairy whipping cream
2 T instant coffee
2 T dark brown sugar

1. Grease generously two round 8 inch cake pans. Line with waxed paper. Grease again and then flour.

2. Beat whites until foamy. Add vanilla and vinegar. Slowly add sugar, beating constantly until mixture is stiff.

3. Gently fold in nuts and pour into prepared cake pans.

4. Bake in a 375° oven for 30 minutes. When cool, remove from pan.

5. Combine the non-dairy whipping cream, instant coffee and sugar and whip stiff. Fill and frost cakes.

This is best made one day in advance.

sunshine cake

1 C sugar
3 eggs, beaten
1 T grated orange peel
⅓ C orange juice
2 t grated lemon peel
2 T lemon juice
pinch salt
1 C non-dairy whipping cream
1 sponge cake
½ orange, sliced very thin

1. Combine first 7 ingredients in top of double boiler. Cook, stirring constantly, until thick.

2. Chill in refrigerator overnight, or for at least 4 hours.

3. Whip the non-dairy whipping cream until stiff. Fold into chilled orange mixture.

4. Split sponge cake into four layers. Fill and frost top and sides with chilled mixture.

5. Garnish with thinly sliced orange.

scotch cake

2 T unflavored gelatin
1 C cold water
6 eggs, separated
½ C Scotch whiskey
1 C sugar
1 t lemon juice
2 C non-dairy whipping cream,
     whipped stiff
3 pkg. lady fingers, split

1. Sprinkle gelatin over cold water. Allow to stand 5 minutes. Heat gelatin over hot water until dissolved; set aside.

2. Beat egg yolks until pale yellow. Add Scotch very slowly, beating well. Beat in sugar and lemon juice.

3. Blend in gelatin mixture and chill slightly.

4. Fold in whipped non-dairy whipping cream.

5. Beat egg whites stiff and fold into gelatin mixture.

6. Line sides and bottom of a 12 inch spring form pan with split lady fingers, round side out.

7. Pour in half of the mixture. Top with another layer of lady fingers. Pour in remaining mixture. Arrange a design of lady fingers on top.

The distinctive taste of Scotch is completely disguised. The end result is a tasty dessert that intrigues guests with its unique flavor.

zuppa inglese

     5 **eggs, separated**
  1½ **C sugar**
  1½ **C flour**
     1 **t vanilla**
     ½ **t grated lemon peel**
     ½ **C sherry**
     1 **recipe Chocolate-Vanilla Custard**
     ¼ **C rum**
     ¼ **C brandy**
        grated chocolate

1. Beat egg yolks with sugar until pale yellow.

2. Beat egg whites stiff. Fold whites into yolks.

3. Sift flour 3 times. Slowly fold it into the batter. Fold in vanilla and lemon peel.

4. Grease and flour 2 round 9 inch cake pans. Pour in batter. Bake in a 350° oven for 20 minutes. Cool cakes on wire rack.

5. Cut each layer in half, yielding 4 layers.

6. Place one layer of cake on serving plate. Sprinkle with ¼ cup sherry. Spread half of the chocolate custard on this layer.

7. Place second cake layer on, crust side down. Sprinkle with ¼ cup rum. Spread half the vanilla custard on this layer.

8. Place on the third cake layer, crust side down, and sprinkle with ¼ cup brandy. Spread on remaining chocolate custard.

9. Sprinkle the cut side of the fourth layer with ¼ cup sherry and place layer with crust side up. Spread with remaining vanilla custard.

10. Sprinkle with grated chocolate and refrigerate overnight.

chocolate-vanilla custard

4 T sugar
4 egg yolks
4 T flour
2⅔ C liquid non-dairy creamer
1 t vanilla
1 t grated lemon peel
2 oz. unsweetened chocolate

1. Stir together sugar, egg yolks and flour. Set aside.

2. Heat non-dairy creamer to just below the boiling point. Pour this very slowly into egg mixture, stirring constantly over medium heat. Cook until thickened. Add vanilla.

3. Divide mixture in half. To one half add the lemon peel. To the other half add the chocolate and continue to cook until chocolate is melted. Cover and cool both mixtures.

sacher torte

2 8″ layers of chocolate cake
3 T boiling water
¾ C currant jelly
6 oz. chocolate chips
1 T shortening
3 T light corn syrup
2 T liquid non-dairy creamer
   almonds, sliced

1. Cut cakes in half, yielding 4 layers.

2. Add water to jelly and beat until smooth.

3. Spread some jelly on top of the cake layers. Stack on a serving platter.

4. Spread remaining jelly on sides of cake. Chill.

5. Melt the chocolate and shortening over hot water. Remove from heat and add corn syrup and non-dairy creamer. Mix well.

6. Pour warm frosting over chilled torte. Garnish with sliced almonds.

saucey chocolate fudge cake

1 C flour
1 t salt
½ C liquid non-dairy creamer
1 t vanilla
6 T cocoa
2 t baking powder
⅔ C sugar
2 T margarine, melted
½ C nuts
1 C brown sugar
1½ C boiling water

1. Combine flour, salt, non-dairy creamer, vanilla, 2 tablespoons cocoa, baking powder, sugar and melted margarine. Mix together well. Stir in nuts.

2. Pour into a greased 1 quart baking dish.

3. Mix brown sugar with remaining cocoa and sprinkle over batter.

4. Pour boiling water over top.

5. Bake in a 350° oven for 40 minutes.

   Serve warm or cold.

This cake creates its own sauce.

no bake chocolate souffle

6 eggs, separated
2 pkg. lady fingers, split
12 oz. chocolate chips
4 T sugar
6 T cold water
½ t salt
½ t vanilla
½ t almond extract
1 T rum
1 C non-dairy whipping cream,
    whipped stiff
   chocolate curls

1. Beat egg yolks. Set aside.

2. Line sides and bottom of spring form pan with lady fingers, round side out; press down on bottom of pan. Set aside.

3. Combine chocolate chips, sugar and water and melt over low heat; cool.

4. Stir in beaten egg yolks and chill.

5. Add salt, vanilla, almond and rum.

6. Beat egg whites stiff. Fold egg whites and non-dairy whipping cream into egg yolk mixture.

7. Pour into prepared pan.

8. Garnish with chocolate curls.

9. Chill in refrigerator overnight.

chocolate mayonnaise cake

3 C flour
1½ C sugar
⅓ C cocoa
2¼ t baking powder
1½ t baking soda
1½ C mayonnaise
1½ C water
1½ t vanilla
1 recipe Chocolate Cream Filling
1 recipe Chocolate Frosting

1. Sift dry ingredients together.

2. Stir in mayonnaise.

3. Gradually stir in water and vanilla and blend until smooth.

4. Grease two 9″ cake pans. Line bottoms with waxed paper.

5. Pour batter into prepared cake pans. Bake in 350° oven for 30 minutes.

6. Fill cake with **Chocolate Cream Filling** and frost with **Chocolate Frosting**.

chocolate frosting

1 oz. unsweetened chocolate
2 T margarine
1 egg white
2 t cold water
⅔ C confectioners sugar
½ t vanilla

1. Melt chocolate and margarine together very slowly. Cool.

2. Beat egg white and water together; add sugar and vanilla and beat until stiff.

3. Fold whites into chocolate mixture, mixing just enough to blend. Spread on cake immediately.

chocolate cream filling

1½ C liquid non-dairy creamer
1 oz. unsweetened chocolate
⅓ C flour
½ C sugar
⅛ t salt
1 egg yolk
2 T margarine
½ t vanilla

1. Melt chocolate in non-dairy creamer slowly; then bring to just below the boiling point.

2. Combine flour, sugar and salt. Gradually add the hot liquid.

3. Cook over medium heat until thick, stirring constantly. Cover and cook 15 minutes. Remove from heat.

4. Temper egg yolk and add to remaining hot mixture. Add margarine. Stir and cook 1 minute more. Remove from heat; cool and then stir in vanilla.

torte au chocolate

         2 C walnuts, finely ground
         8 eggs, extra large
     1½ C sugar
         2 T vanilla
         4 T flour
         5 t baking powder
         4 T cocoa
         1 recipe Chocolate Cloud Frosting

1. Beat eggs; add walnuts.

2. Add remaining ingredients except frosting and mix well.

3. Grease and flour two 10″ spring form pans. Pour in batter. Bake in a 350° oven for 20 minutes.

4. Refrigerate cake in pan for 1 hour. Remove from pans.

5. Split each layer in half. (It will fall apart as you cut. However, as you frost you can put it together.)

6. Fill and frost with **Chocolate Cloud Frosting.**

chocolate cloud frosting

     2 C non-dairy whipping cream
     ¾ C chocolate syrup

Combine ingredients and whip stiff.

chocolate sponge cake

6 eggs, separated
1 C sugar
1 C chocolate syrup
1 T vanilla
1 T very hot water
1 C self-rising flour
1 recipe Chocolate Cloud Frosting

1. Beat egg yolks until thick. Add sugar gradually.

2. Combine chocolate syrup, vanilla and water.

3. Add flour and liquid alternately to egg yolk mixture.

4. Beat egg whites stiff. Fold into egg yolk mixture.

5. Bake in a 10″ tube pan in a 350° oven for 50-60 minutes.

6. Invert pan and cool.

7. Split into three layers; fill and frost with **Chocolate Cloud Frosting**.

easy fruit cake

1 can cherry pie filling
1 lb. 4 oz. can crushed pineapple,
     including syrup
1 box yellow cake mix
1 C walnuts, chopped
1 C shredded coconut
1 C margarine, melted

1. Spread cherry pie filling into a 9 x 13″ pan.
2. Over this, pour pineapple; then sprinkle on cake mix, nuts and lastly, coconut.
3. Pour the melted margarine over all.
4. Bake in a 350° oven for 45 minutes, until golden brown.
5. Cool in pan; cut into squares to serve.

cranberry spice cake

½ C shortening
1 C sugar
1 egg, beaten
1 C raisins
½ C nuts
1¾ C flour
¼ t salt
1 t baking soda
1 t baking powder
1 t cinnamon
½ t cloves
1 C cranberry sauce, jellied or whole

1. Cream shortening and sugar; add egg.
2. Stir in raisins and nuts.
3. Add dry ingredients.
4. Stir in cranberry sauce.
5. Pour into a greased 9 inch tube pan.
6. Bake in a 350° oven for 1 hour.

boston cream pie

1   egg
½   C sugar
2   T margarine, melted
1   C flour
1   t baking powder
⅛   t salt
⅓   C liquid non-dairy creamer
1   recipe Custard Filling
¼   C cocoa
1¼   C confectioners sugar
¼   C margarine
2   T orange juice

1. Grease one round 9 inch cake pan. Line it with waxed paper. Grease it again and then flour it. Set aside.

2. Beat egg and sugar together. Add melted margarine.

3. Sift together the flour, baking powder and salt. Add to egg mixture alternately with non-dairy creamer.

4. Pour into prepared pan.

5. Bake in a 375° oven for 25 minutes.

6. Cool; slice into 2 layers. Place on cake plate.

7. Fill cake with **Custard Filling**.

8. Combine cocoa and confectioners sugar.

9. Melt margarine in orange juice. Remove from heat.

10. Blend together orange juice and cocoa mixture to make glaze.

11. Pour warm glaze over cake. Allow to cool and serve.

custard filling

⅓   C sugar
½   T flour
1   T cornstarch
⅛   t salt
1   egg
1   C liquid non-dairy creamer
1   t vanilla

1. Mix together dry ingredients.

2. Add egg and non-dairy creamer. Stir until blended.

3. Cook, stirring, until thick, about 5 minutes.

4. Remove from heat and add vanilla. Cool.

almond puff

- **1 C margarine**
- **2 C flour**
- **2 T water**
- **1 C water**
- **1 t almond extract**
- **3 eggs**
- **1 recipe Almond Glaze**
- **sliced almonds**

1. Cut ½ cup margarine into 1 cup flour. Sprinkle with 2 tablespoons water. Mix with a fork.

2. Roll into a ball. Divide in half.

3. On an ungreased baking sheet, pat each half into a 12 x 3″ strip. Place strips 3 inches apart.

4. Heat ½ cup margarine and 1 cup water to a rolling boil. Remove from heat. Stir in almond extract and 1 cup flour. Stir vigorously over low heat until mixture forms a ball. Remove from heat; cool slightly.

5. Beat in eggs, one at a time, until smooth.

6. Divide this mixture in half and spread evenly over strips on baking sheet, completely covering strips.

7. Bake in a 350° oven for 1 hour. Cool.

8. Frost with **Almond Glaze** and sprinkle with nuts.

almond glaze

- **1½ C confectioners sugar**
- **2 T margarine**
- **1½ t almond extract**
- **2 T warm water**

Beat all together until smooth, just before using.

linzertorte

¾ C margarine
½ C sugar
1 egg yolk
1 t grated lemon peel
1⅓ C flour
½ t cinnamon
¼ t cloves
¼ t nutmeg
3 oz. hazel nuts, ground fine
¾ C currant jelly
¼ C raspberry jam
1 egg yolk mixed with ½ t water
   sliced almonds
   confectioners sugar

1. Cream margarine with sugar. Add egg yolk and beat until light and fluffy. Add lemon peel.

2. Combine spices with flour; add alternately with ground nuts to the batter. Chill dough 15 minutes.

3. Grease and flour a 9″ pan. Press ⅔ of the dough into the bottom of the pan and ¼ inch up the side.

4. Combine currant jelly and raspberry jam. Spread mixture over dough.

5. Roll remaining dough into strips and put on top of jam in a criss-cross pattern and then around the perimeter.

6. Brush with egg yolk mixture and sprinkle with sliced almonds.

7. Bake in a 375° oven for 35 minutes.

8. Freeze in pan for 1 hour and then remove from pan.

9. Dust with confectioners sugar before serving.

flaky pastry

3 C flour
¼ t salt
1 C vegetable shortening
⅓ C orange juice

1. Mix flour and salt together.

2. Cut shortening into flour until pea size pieces are formed.

3. Add orange juice, a little at a time, tossing dough with a fork, until the dough holds together to form a ball.

4. Lightly shape into a round and chill for 30 minutes.

5. Flatten pastry slightly into desired shape (round, rectangle). Roll out on a lightly floured board.

6. When using this pastry in a pie shell, prick bottom and sides well with a fork. Next, place a layer of uncooked, dried beans over waxed paper in the shell, to minimize shrinkage.

   Bake in a 400° oven for 10 minutes, or until lightly browned. Discard paper; reserve beans to use again. Cool pie shell before filling.

A pastry blender is recommended for cutting shortening into flour. If this gadget is not in your kitchen, improvise with 2 table knives, using one in each hand.

rich sweet pastry

1½ C flour, sifted
½ C margarine, cut into 16 pieces
¼ t salt
1 egg yolk
1 T lemon juice
2 T sugar
   ice water, if needed
   egg white, lightly beaten

1. Mound flour on a board. Make a well in the center of the flour. Into the well, place cut up margarine, egg yolk, salt, lemon juice and sugar.

2. From the outside in, work the mixture together until blended, with your finger tips. Add water only if needed to hold mixture together.

3. Fraiser dough by taking a small piece of the dough mixture and sliding it across a board with the heel of your hand. When all the dough has been used, reform it into a ball and repeat the operation.

4. Wrap in waxed paper and refrigerate 30 minutes.

5. Roll out dough between 2 sheets of waxed paper. Line a 9 inch tart pan with the pastry.

6. Prick bottom and sides well with a fork. Next, place a layer of uncooked, dried beans over waxed paper in the shell, to minimize shrinkage.

7. Bake in a 425° oven for 15 minutes. Brush with lightly beaten egg whites and bake an additional 5 minutes.

glazed peach tart

¾ C sugar
½ C margarine, melted
2 eggs
2½ C flour
½ t baking powder
2 t grated lemon peel
   bread crumbs
1 lb. 13 oz. can sliced peaches,
      drained
12 oz. jar peach preserves
¼ t cinnamon
¼ t nutmeg

1. Combine sugar, margarine and eggs.

2. Add flour, baking powder and lemon peel. Mix together until a ball is formed. Reserve a quarter of ball for top crust.

3. Roll dough into 12 inch circle, ½ inch thick. Place into a 12 inch tart pan and work up the sides with fingertips.

4. Sprinkle lightly with bread crumbs. Spread peaches in one layer on pastry.

5. Mix spices with preserves; spread over peaches.

6. Roll out reserved dough. Cut into ½ inch strips. Place strips in a lattice pattern over filling.

7. Bake in a 400° oven for 30 minutes.

blueberry tarts

2 pts. blueberries
1 C sugar
¼ C water
1½ T cornstarch
1½ T lemon juice
   pinch salt
2 T light rum
6 tart shells, baked
1 C non-dairy whipping cream, whipped stiff

1. Place one pint of berries in a saucepan with sugar, water, cornstarch, lemon juice, rum and salt.

2. Cook over medium heat until thick and clear, stirring occasionally. Remove from heat and cool.

3. Fold in second pint of uncooked berries.

4. Spoon into baked tart shells. Chill for 5 hours.

5. Just before serving, top with a dollop of whipped topping.

glazed strawberry tart

3 C fresh whole strawberries
½ C currant jelly
2 t orange juice
1 recipe Rich Sweet Pastry, baked

1. Fill cooled tart shell with strawberries, placing strawberries in one layer, points up.

2. Combine currant jelly and orange juice and cook over very low heat until melted. Cool slightly.

3. Pour melted jelly over strawberries and chill.

grasshopper pie

24 marshmallows
½ C liquid non-dairy creamer
4 T green creme de menthe
2 t white creme de cacao
1 C liquid non-dairy whipping cream, whipped stiff
1 recipe Cocoa Pie Crust

1. Melt marshmallows in liquid non-dairy creamer. Cool.

2. Stir in creme de menthe and creme de cacao.

3. Fold in whipped non-dairy whipping cream.

4. Pour into prepared pie crust.

5. Chill overnight.

cocoa pie crust

1 C flour
¼ C cocoa
2 T sugar
½ t salt
⅓ C shortening
3 T liquid non-dairy creamer
½ t vanilla

1. Combine dry ingredients.

2. Cut in shortening.

3. Stir in non-dairy creamer and vanilla.

4. Roll between 2 pieces of wax paper; do not add flour.

5. Place in 8″ pie plate. Prick and bake in a 400° oven for 10 minutes.

glamourous strawberry pie

2 egg whites
½ t vinegar
¼ t salt
⅓ C sugar
9″ pie shell, baked
2 C fresh strawberries, sliced
¼ C sugar
1 t cornstarch
½ C water
½ t strawberry extract
½ C non-dairy whipping cream

1. Beat egg whites with vinegar and salt until foamy. Add ⅓ cup sugar and beat until stiff.

2. Spread beaten egg whites on bottom and sides of pie shell. Bake in a 325° oven for 12 minutes. Cool.

3. Mash ½ cup berries with ¼ cup sugar.

4. Combine cornstarch and water and stir into berries. Cook and continue stirring until mixture boils. Cook 2 minutes. Stir in remaining berries. Cool.

5. Spread this mixture over meringue and chill.

6. Combine strawberry extract and non-dairy whipping cream. Whip until stiff. Spread over strawberry filling and serve.

black bottom pie

  2 t unflavored gelatin
  ¼ C cold water
  1 C sugar
  2 T cornstarch
  ⅛ t salt
  2¾ C liquid non-dairy creamer
  2 egg yolks, slightly beaten
  1 T rum
  2 oz. unsweetened chocolate
  1 t vanilla
  9″ pie shell, baked
  2 egg whites
  ⅓ C shredded coconut, toasted

1. Sprinkle gelatin over cold water. Allow to stand for 5 minutes.

2. Combine ¾ cup sugar, cornstarch, salt and non-dairy creamer. Mix well. Bring to a boil, stirring constantly. Temper egg yolks. Then stir egg yolks into this hot mixture. Cook 1 minute longer.

3. Measure 1½ cups of this mixture into a bowl. Stir in gelatin mixture. Add rum. Chill until thickened.

4. Add chocolate and 2 tablespoons sugar to remaining hot mixture. Place over heat and stir until chocolate is melted and blended. Remove from heat and stir in vanilla. Cool slightly. Pour into pie shell and chill.

5. Beat egg whites until foamy. Add 2 tablespoons sugar and beat until soft peaks form. Fold egg whites into chilled rum mixture.

6. Spoon this mixture over chilled chocolate mixture. Refrigerate to set.

7. At serving time, sprinkle with toasted coconut.

pumpkin chiffon pie

2 C canned pumpkin
3 egg yolks, beaten
1 C liquid non-dairy creamer
¾ C sugar
½ t salt
1 t cinnamon
½ t ginger
¼ t nutmeg
3 egg whites, beaten stiff
9″ pie shell, unbaked

1. Combine pumpkin, egg yolks, non-dairy creamer, sugar, salt, cinnamon, ginger and nutmeg.

2. Fold egg whites into pumpkin mixture.

3. Pour batter into unbaked pie shell.

4. Bake in a 450° oven for 10 minutes; reduce temperature to 325° and continue baking for 45 minutes.

Egg whites should be beaten until peaks hold and are moist, but not wet. Carefully turn the filled bowl upside down. If whites are the proper consistency they will remain in the bowl. Small children squeal with delight when this test is performed over one's head.

colonial apple pie

3 lbs. McIntosh apples, sliced
¾ C quick cooking oatmeal
¾ C brown sugar
½ C flour
¼ t salt
½ C margarine
⅓ C walnuts, coarsely chopped

1. Mound apples in a 9 inch pie plate.

2. Combine oatmeal, sugar, flour, salt. Cut margarine into this mixture. Add nuts.

3. Pat mixture over apples.

4. Bake in a 375° oven for 40 minutes. Serve warm.

pecan pie

2 C sugar
1 C dark corn syrup
3 T margarine
½ t salt
1 t vanilla
4 eggs, slightly beaten
5 oz. pecans
10″ pie shell, unbaked

1. Heat sugar and corn syrup until sugar is dissolved and mixture comes to a slow boil. Remove from heat.

2. Add margarine and stir until melted.

3. Add salt and vanilla.

4. Temper eggs and then add eggs to hot syrup mixture.

5. Add nuts; stir well.

6. Pour into unbaked pie shell.

7. Bake in a 425° oven for 10 minutes; reduce temperature to 375° and continue baking for 35 minutes.

sweet potato pie

5 canned sweet potatoes, mashed
2 eggs, beaten
⅓ C liquid non-dairy creamer
1 t vanilla
¼ C margarine, melted
¼ t cinnamon
¼ t nutmeg
⅓ C brown sugar
8″ pie shell, unbaked

1. Combine first 8 ingredients and mix until smooth.

2. Pour into unbaked pie shell.

3. Bake in a 350° oven for 30 minutes.

french silk pie

¼ lb. margarine
¾ C sugar
1 oz. unsweetened chocolate, melted
1 t vanilla
2 eggs
8″ pie shell, baked

1. Cream margarine and gradually add sugar.
2. Add chocolate and vanilla. Beat well.
3. Add 1 egg and beat 5 minutes.
4. Add second egg and beat another 5 minutes.
5. Pour into pie shell. Refrigerate overnight.

Excessive beating is the secret of making this pie as smooth as silk.

avocado mousse

3 ripe avocados
1½ C liquid non-dairy creamer
1 C sugar
½ C lemon juice
1 t vanilla
2 C non-dairy whipping cream, whipped stiff
¼ t lemon extract
2 t grated lemon peel

1. Puree together avocados, non-dairy creamer, sugar, lemon juice and vanilla.

2. Fold in 1 cup whipped non-dairy whipping cream. Spoon into 12 individual serving glasses. Cover with plastic wrap and refrigerate overnight.

3. Mix remaining whipped non-dairy creamer with lemon extract. Spoon on top of avocado mixture; garnish with lemon peel and serve.

bananas flambe

5 T sugar
4 T margarine
½ C orange juice
2 T orange flavored liqueur
4 bananas, split lengthwise
2 T cognac

1. Melt sugar until lightly browned.

2. Add margarine, orange juice and orange liqueur. Simmer until creamy.

3. Place bananas in sauce and cook 3 minutes.

4. Pour cognac over bananas and flame.

The red food coloring should be omitted from the **Non-Dairy Ice Cream** *recipe, should it be served in combination with* **Bananas Flambe**.

cranberry cobbler

1 C sugar
½ t cinnamon
½ C orange juice
2 C cranberries
7 slices fresh white bread
½ C margarine, melted

1. Mix sugar and cinnamon with orange juice. Bring to a boil and stir until dissolved.
2. Add cranberries and cook rapidly for 2 minutes.
3. Trim crusts from bread. Make fluffly bread crumbs in blender or food processor. Toss with melted margarine.
4. In a 1½ quart greased baking dish, sprinkle a layer of crumbs. Spoon on a layer of cranberry mixture. Continue layers, ending with crumbs.
5. Cover and bake in a 375° oven for 20 minutes. Remove cover and bake 15 minutes longer or until top is brown and crunchy.

crystal oranges

6 navel oranges, peeled, sliced
11 oz. can Mandarin oranges, drained
⅓ C orange marmalade
3 T orange flavored liqueur

1. Combine oranges in a bowl.
2. Combine marmalade with liqueur.
3. Pour marmalade mixture over oranges and steep overnight in refrigerator.
4. Serve very cold.

clafouti aux peches

⅔ C sugar
¼ C orange flavored liqueur
2 C sliced peaches
1 C liquid non-dairy creamer
1 T vanilla
3 eggs
⅛ t salt
⅔ C flour
   confectioners sugar

1. Dissolve ⅓ cup sugar in orange flavored liqueur. Add peaches and arrange this mixture in a generously greased 1½ quart baking dish. Set aside.

2. Blend until smooth the liquid non-dairy creamer, remaining sugar, vanilla, eggs, salt and flour.

3. Carefully pour this batter over the fruit.

4. Bake in a 350° oven for 45 minutes.

5. Sprinkle top with confectioners sugar and serve hot or warm.

cherry cloud

1 C liquid non-dairy whipping cream, whipped stiff
1 T cherry liqueur
5 oz. minature marshmallows, quartered
10″ pie shell, baked
1 lb. 6 oz. can cherry pie filling

1. Combine whipped non-dairy creamer, cherry liqueur and marshmallows.

2. Layer half of this mixture in pie shell. Cover with pie filling. Top with remaining marshmallow mixture. Chill and serve.

rhubarb brown betty

1½ C sugar
 3 T flour
 ¼ t salt
 1 T lemon juice
 2 eggs, beaten
 1 T margarine
 4 C rhubarb, cut into ½'' pieces
 ¾ C sugar
 ½ C flour
 2 t grated orange peel
 ⅓ C margarine, softened

1. Combine first 7 ingredients. Pour into an 8x8x2'' pan.

2. Mix remaining ingredients together until crumbly. Sprinkle over rhubarb mixture.

3. Bake in a 375° oven for 45 minutes. Serve warm or cold.

windy city pineapple blocks

 8 oz. vanilla wafers, crushed
 1 C margarine
1½ C confectioners sugar
 2 eggs
 1 C non-dairy whipping cream, whipped stiff
8½ oz. can crushed pineapple, drained

1. Spread half of the crushed wafers in the bottom of a 13x8x2'' greased pan.

2. Cream margarine and sugar together. Add eggs and beat well. Spread this mixture over crumbs.

3. Combine whipped non-dairy whipping cream and pineapple. Spread over mixture in pan.

4. Top with remaining wafer crumbs and refrigerate overnight.

5. Cut into squares to serve.

mango mousse

5 lbs. mangoes, peeled
⅓ C lime juice
2 T dark rum
2 egg whites
   pinch salt
⅓ C sugar
½ C non-dairy whipping cream,
   whipped stiff

1. Cut 2 mangoes into ¼ inch dice. Reserve.

2. Puree remaining mangoes. Stir in lime juice and rum.

3. Beat egg whites with salt and sugar until stiff.

4. Fold egg whites into the whipped non-dairy whipping cream. Fold gently into the mango puree. Fold in the diced mango.

5. Spoon into a glass serving bowl or individual serving glasses.

6. Refrigerate 3 hours.

heavenly ambrosia

2 eggs
1 C sugar
8 oz. whole dates, cut into thirds
1¼ C walnuts, coarsely chopped
2 T flour
2 t baking powder
1 t vanilla

1. Beat eggs at high speed, add sugar slowly.

2. Fold in remaining ingredients.

3. Pour into 2 quart casserole.

4. Bake in a 300° oven for 50 minutes. Serve warm.

This dessert baffles everyone. The date flavor is unpronounced; the ingredients are blended into a very rich confection and the final result is a treat for those with a sweet tooth.

CHINESE COOKERY

Chinese people do not eat in courses as we do. Their meal is served all together, all the dishes being placed on the table at the same time and guests then helping themselves. Even soup is not served separately as a course, but included rather as a beverage.

However, when planning a Chinese dinner party, we suggest you arrange it Western style with appetizers served first, followed by soup and then the main course. It is customary to serve one main dish for every two guests seated at the table. Choose dishes that will offer variety to your guests: one chicken dish, one beef, one a rice or noodle dish. Also vary your selection to include a stir-fry, a deep-fry, a hot Szechuen dish, one without a sauce, etc. In other words, when planning a menu for a party of six, decide on your appetizer and soup. Then choose one dish from column A, one from column B, and one from column C.

A

Szechuen Chicken
Sweet and Sour Chicken
Chicken with Mushrooms
Chicken with Hoisin Sauce
Chicken with Cucumbers
Chicken Cantonese
Fried Chicken with Walnuts
Deep-Fried Chicken Legs
Black Satin Chicken
Lemon Chicken I, II
Chicken Salad
Sesame Chicken Salad
Szechuen Chicken Salad
Moo Sho Roo
Peking Duck
Steamed Duck

B

White Rice
Fried Rice
Golden Fried Rice
Fried Rice Stick
Vegetables and Soft Noodles
Fried Noodles
Fried Noodle Plate
Egg Foo Yung Sub Gum
Brocolli, Mushrooms,
   Water Chestnuts
Garlic Spinach
Asparagus Salad
Green Beans

C

Beef, Broccoli,
   Black Beans
Beef and Snow Peas
Steak Kew
Beef with String Beans
Beef, Snow Peas,
   Baby Corn
Stuffed Cucumber
Red Simmered Beef
Pearl Meat Balls
Steamed Meat with Taro

chinese glossary

AGAR-AGAR is a dried seaweed which resembles transparent noodles. It acts like unflavored gelatin when soaked in hot water. When soaked in cold water, it serves as noodles.

BEAN CURD is pureed soy beans which have been pressed into a cake. Also available is brown bean curd, which has been flavored.

BOK CHOY is Chinese cabbage.

CHINESE CABBAGE is also known as celery cabbage.

CHINESE MUSHROOMS are black dried mushrooms from the Orient. Soak before using, squeeze dry, discard stems.

FERMENTED BLACK BEANS are preserved soy beans, very strongly flavored and salty.

FIVE SPICE POWDER is a combination of five spices available in one bottle, (star anise, anise pepper, fennel, cloves, cinnamon).

HOISIN SAUCE is a sweet and spicy sauce made from soy beans, spices, garlic and chili.

HOT OIL can be purchased or prepared at home. Place one chili pepper into one cup of corn oil.

LILY BUDS are dried lily flowers. Measure dry and then soak before using.

RED BEAN PASTE is a sweetened puree of Chinese red beans. It is available in cans.

SESAME OIL is made from toasted white sesame seeds. It should be used sparingly.

STAR ANISE is an eight-pointed brown seeded cluster. It adds a licorice like flavor. Eight pods count as one star.

STEAMING in the Chinese manner is wet steaming, or cooking in a chamber of live steam. There are many different steaming set-ups available, or one may devise one's own. But, please do not confuse this with the double-boiler method of dry steaming.

SZECHUEN PEPPERCORNS are hot brown peppercorns.

TREE EARS are dried fungi. It is measured dry and then soaked before using.

WOK, a large skillet or an electric fry pan may be used interchangeably.

instructions

Before you begin cooking a Chinese recipe, please do the following:

1. Reduce all ingredients to a state of readiness by preparing them according to description, i.e. diced, shredded, blanched, marinated, etc.
2. In separate bowls, line up the prepared ingredients in the order in which they are to be used. Place within easy reach of the wok. Ingredients grouped together in the recipe can be combined in the same bowl.
3. Then, and only then, proceed to cook.

five spice balls
heung hew fun

1. Soak in hot water to cover, 20 minutes:

   ¼ **C bulghur**

2. Combine softened bulghur with:

   2 C chick peas, mashed

   3 T bread crumbs

   1 egg

   8 water chestnuts, minced

   2 t five spice powder

   ¼ **t salt**

   Chill in refrigerator for 15 minutes.

3. Shape into 12-16 balls.

4. Roll balls in:

   cornstarch

5. Heat in wok to 375°:

   2 C oil

6. Deep-fry coated balls until golden.

exotic bamboo tray

1. Place into sauce pot:

   1 qt. water

   3 T sherry

   1 T salt

   1 C soy sauce

   2 T sugar

   3 pieces ginger root

   2 scallions

   12 oz. can whole bamboo shoots

   1 spice bag:

     2 star anise

     ¼ stick cinnamon

     ½ t Szechuen peppercorns

     ¼ t five spice powder

   1 lb. brisket, rolled, tied securely

   ½ chicken, pullet or roaster

   ½ lb. chicken gizzards

2. Bring to a boil, reduce heat and simmer for 2 hours.

3. Remove and chill cooked meats, poultry and bamboo shoots. Reserve stock. Discard spice bag.

4. Add to stock in pot:

   6 hard cooked eggs, shelled

   2 cakes brown bean curd

   Cook for 30 minutes.

5. Remove bean curd and refrigerate.

   Refrigerate eggs in stock overnight.

6. To serve: slice all except eggs thinly. Arrange on platter with quartered eggs.

The eggs have taken on the color of the stock. Brown eggs on a bamboo tray, accompanied by thinly sliced, and thus disguised, chicken gizzards, etc. is sure to start your party off at an exotic pace.

Leftovers will hold in the refrigerator one week. The sauce may also be held for reuse, in a covered jar, after discarding the scallion and ginger root.

lamb riblets and their sauces

Marinate ribs in a sauce overnight.

Cook, covered, in the sauce for one hour, in a 350° oven.
Remove to rack and brown under broiler.

I

Mix together:
- ½ C soy sauce
- 1 t salt
- 1 T sherry
- 1 t garlic powder
- ½ t ginger powder
- ⅛ t pepper
- ¼ t five spice powder
- 3 T sugar
- 1 T sesame oil

II

Mix together:
- 3 scallions, chopped
- 3 pieces ginger root, minced
- 5 T soy sauce
- 1 T sherry
- 2 T sugar
- 3 T hoisin sauce
- 1 T sesame oil
- 1 T hot water

III

Mix together:
- 2 T honey
- 4 slices ginger root, minced
- 2 scallions, chopped
- 4 T sherry
- 2 cloves garlic, minced
- 2 T hoisin sauce
- 2 T soy sauce
- 2 T chili sauce
- 2 T catsup
- 2 T corn syrup
- ½ t salt

chicken fingers

1. Mix together to make batter:
   2 t baking powder
   1 C cold water
   1 C flour
   6 T oil
   1 t sherry

2. Dip into the batter:
   1 lb. chicken cutlets, cut into
   **   ½ x 3″ pieces**

3. Heat in wok to 375°:
   2 C oil

4. Add and deep-fry the chicken until golden.

5. Serve with **Loquat Sauce.**

loquat sauce

1. Mix together in a small covered container:
   1 t soy sauce
   2 T cornstarch
   2 T water
   Shake well and set aside.

2. Combine in a sauce pan:
   1 C loquat juice (liquid from canned
   **   loquats)**
   1 T peanut oil
   2½ T lemon juice
   1½ T sugar
   1 t sherry
   Bring to a boil.

3. Add to saucepan:
   ½ C chicken broth
   Return to boil.

4. Stirring constantly, add cornstarch mixture and return to a boil.

This sauce combines well with many deep-fried batter dishes that have no sauce of their own.

To reheat this sauce, place it over very, very low heat and allow it to reach the boiling point without stirring.

fried chicken wings

1. Mix together to make batter:
   ½ C flour
   1 T cornstarch
   1 egg
   ½ t baking powder
   1 t salt
   ½ C water

2. Dip into batter:
   1 lb. chicken wings, cut at joints

3. Heat in wok to 375°:
   2 C oil

4. Add and deep-fry the chicken wings until golden.

5. Serve with **Duck Sauce.**

This batter produces a very crispy crust which is not suitable for other dishes.

duck sauce

Mix together:
   1 C apricot preserve
   1 C peach preserve
   1 C applesauce
   2 T catsup
   2 T chili sauce
   2 t dry mustard

This sauce freezes well. It may also be used as a dipping sauce for egg rolls.

wontons

1. Combine to make wonton filling:
   - **1 lb. ground beef**
   - **½ pkg. frozen broccoli, minced**
   - **1 t ginger, minced**
   - **3 T soy sauce**
   - **½ t salt**
   - **1 egg**

2. Place 1 teaspoon of filling on center of:
   - **wonton skin**

   Fold skin in half to make triangle. Bring one set of opposite tips together and seal with one drop of water. Fold sides in and pinch together. It resembles a nurse's cap.

   Keep skins covered with a damp towel at all times.

3. Bring to a boil:
   - **2 qt. water**

4. Add 20 wontons at one time.

5. Bring back to boil and add:
   - **1 C of cold water**

6. Repeat this process 3 times. Then boil for two minutes. Drain.

This recipe will fill approximately 1 lb. of skins. Skins may be purchased at an oriental food store; or follow the recipe for **Egg Roll Skins** *and cut them into 2 inch squares.*

Wontons may be deep-fried to use as appetizers, or boiled to put in soup.

egg roll skins

1. Combine:
   2 C flour
   ¼ t salt
   ½ C ice water
2. Add:
   1 egg, beaten
3. Knead until smooth.

   Cover dough with a damp towel and refrigerate 30 minutes.

4. Place dough on a floured board. Roll out with a rolling pin until paper thin. Cut into desired size triangles.

5. Place 1 spoonful of **Favorite Filling** on bottom edge of longest side of each triangle. Fold in both sides. Roll up.

6. Seal with 1 drop of water.

7. Heat in wok to 375°:
   2 C oil
8. Deep-fry egg rolls until golden.

Egg rolls can be frozen and reheated in a 425° oven. Place them on a rack over a drip pan. If frozen, bake for 40 minutes, and if defrosted, bake for 20 minutes.

favorite filling

I

1. Heat in wok:
   3 T oil

2. Add to wok and stir-fry for 3 minutes:
   2 lbs. shoulder of veal, minced
   4 T soy sauce
   1 t sugar
   1 T cornstarch
   1 scallion, chopped

3. Add to wok:
   2 T oil

4. Add to wok and stir-fry for 1 minute:
   1 lb. Chinese cabbage, shredded
   5 stalks celery, shredded
   ½ lb. bean sprouts
   2 t salt
   6 oz. bamboo shoots, shredded

5. Add, bring to a boil and stir until thick:
   1 T cornstarch dissolved in 1 T water

6. Drain and cool.

II

1. Heat in wok:
   3 T oil

2. Add to wok and stir-fry for 2 minutes:
   3 T soy sauce
   1 t sugar
   1 T cornstarch
   1 scallion, chopped
   2 cakes brown bean curd, diced
   6 Chinese mushrooms, soaked, diced
   6 oz. water chestnuts, diced
   ½ lb. Chinese cabbage, shredded
   ½ lb. scallions, diced

3. Add, bring to a boil, and stir until thick:
   2 T cornstarch dissolved in 1 T water

4. Drain and cool.

III

1. Heat in wok:
   1 T oil

2. Add to wok and stir-fry for 1 minute:
   ½ lb. ground beef

3. Add to wok and mix well:
   1 T sherry
   1 T soy sauce
   ½ t sugar
   4 Chinese mushrooms, soaked,
       shredded

   Set aside.

4. Heat in wok:
   2 T oil

5. Add to wok and stir-fry for 1 minute:
   ½ lb. bean sprouts
   ½ C bamboo shoots, shredded
   1 t salt

6. Add meat mixture and stir-fry 1 minute:

7. Add, bring to a boil, and stir until thick:
   1 T cornstarch dissolved in 2 T water

8. Drain and cool.

rickshaw wheels

1. Mix together:

   ½ t cornstarch

   1½ t water

   ⅛ t salt

2. Add:

   1 egg, well beaten

   Reserve 1 teaspoon of this mixture.

   Set aside.

3. Heat in a 10 inch skillet:

   ½ t oil

4. Pour in egg mixture, making one large, thin pancake. Use reserved egg mixture to fill in any holes which might occur. Cook slowly till done. Remove to cutting board.

5. Mix together:

   4 oz. ground veal

   1 t cornstarch

   1 t sherry

   1 egg

   2 drops red food coloring

6. Spread the veal mixture over the egg pancake. Roll it up and seal the edge with reserved egg mixture.

7. Place in steamer and cook for 15 minutes. Remove and cool. Slice into ¼ inch pieces. Serve cold.

To make two pancakes, double everything but the egg in the veal mixture.

marbled tea eggs

1. Boil for 10 minutes:
   6 eggs

2. Semi-crack each egg gently.

3. Bring to a boil:
   2 C water
   2 tea bags
   2 T soy sauce
   1 star anise seed
   2 T salt
   6 eggs with semi-cracked shells

   Reduce heat and simmer 2 hours. Cool.

4. To serve: remove shells.

Take care to just create fine lines in the shells when semi-cracking them. This allows the cooking liquid to seep through, creating a marbled effect.

soy eggs

1. Bring to a boil:
   2 T soy sauce
   2 T water
   2 t brown sugar
   2 T sherry
   3 hard cooked, shelled eggs

   Simmer 5 minutes. Remove from heat.

2. Steep eggs in sauce for 1½ hours.

3. To serve: quarter eggs.

szechuen pickles

1. Cut into cubes:
   1 lb. cucumbers, peeled

2. Sprinkle with:
   1 T salt

3. Refrigerate 2 to 4 hours. Drain well and pat dry with a paper towel.

4. Mix cucumbers with:
   2 T salt
   3 cloves garlic, smashed
   1 t Szechuen peppercorns
   1 t hot bean paste
   2 T hot oil
   2 t sugar
   1 T vinegar
   2 T sesame oil

5. Drain before serving.

Pickles will keep one week in refrigerator.

smashed radishes

1. Combine:
   1 T soy sauce
   2 T vinegar
   1 t sugar
   ½ t salt

2. Add:
   20 radishes, slightly smashed
   (pound radishes to split but do not break through)

3. Marinate 20 minutes.

   Drain.

4. To serve sprinkle with:
   1 T sesame oil

deep-fried fish

1. Mix together:
   1½ C bleached white flour
   1 T baking powder
   ½ t salt

2. Add and stir in:
   ½ C oil

3. Add slowly, while stirring, to make batter:
   1 C cold water

4. Dip into batter:
   1 lb. sole, cubed

5. Heat in wok to 375°:
   2 C oil

6. Add and deep-fry the fish until golden.

7. Serve with **Apricot Sauce** as appetizer.

The batter should be the consistency of pancake batter. The thicker the batter, the thicker the crust will be. After frying, this batter remains crisp.

Fish can be prepared ahead of time and reheated in the oven before serving.

apricot sauce

Mix together and bring to a boil:
   12 oz. jar apricot jam
   ½ C cider vinegar
   ⅛ t paprika

szechuen fish balls

1. Mix together:
   1 lb. sole, minced
   10 water chestnuts, minced
   1 egg white
   1 t salt
   ½ t sugar
   1 T cornstarch
   1 scallion, minced
   1 slice ginger root, minced
   1 t sherry

2. Shape into 1 inch balls.

3. Heat in wok to 375°:
   2 C oil

4. Deep-fry until golden and set aside.

5. Heat in wok:
   3 T oil

6. Add and stir-fry for one minute:
   2 scallions, minced
   2 T ginger root, minced
   2 cloves garlic, minced

7. Add the deep-fried fish balls to wok and heat through.

8. Add to wok and stir-fry for 2 minutes:
   1 T sherry
   1 T soy sauce
   ½ t salt
   1 t sugar
   ¼ t red pepper

9. Add and mix well:
   ¼ C catsup
   ¼ C chili sauce

10. Serve hot as an appetizer.

fish balls

1. Mix together:
   1 lb. sole, minced
   10 water chestnuts, minced
   1 egg white
   1 t salt
   ½ t sugar
   1 T cornstarch
   2 scallions, minced
   2 slices ginger root, minced
   1 t sherry

2. Shape into 30 balls.

3. Roll balls in:
   cornstarch

4. Heat in wok to 375°:
   2 C oil

5. Deep-fry coated fish balls until golden.

Balls can be made ahead, frozen and re-heated in a 400° oven for 5 minutes.

stuffed mushrooms on lettuce
dong koo min

1. Rinse and soak in warm water for 20 minutes:
   10 large Chinese mushrooms

   Remove; reserve liquid.

   Remove and discard stems from mushrooms.

2. Heat in wok:
   2 T oil

3. Add to wok and stir-fry for 4 minutes:
   10 prepared Chinese mushrooms

4. Add to 1 cup reserved liquid:
   1 t sugar
   1 T soy sauce

   Simmer for 20 minutes.

   Remove mushrooms to warm plate; reserve cooking liquid.

5. Mix together to make stuffing:
   ½ lb. sole, minced
   1 unbeaten egg white
   ½ t ginger juice
   1 t sherry
   1 t cornstarch
   ½ t salt

6. Stuff mushrooms with fish stuffing.

7. Steam stuffed mushrooms 10 minutes.

   Set aside.

8. Heat in wok:
   3 T oil

9. Add to wok and stir-fry till browned:
   1 clove garlic, smashed

   Remove garlic.

10. Add and stir-fry 1 minute:

    1 t salt
    **1 head lettuce, separated, well-
        drained**

    Remove to serving platter.

11. Place mushrooms on lettuce bed.

12. Mix together with reserved cooking
    liquid to make sauce:

    1 T cornstarch
    1 T sherry

    Bring to a boil. Stir to thicken.

13. To serve: pour sauce over all.

*Squeeze ginger in a garlic press to obtain
ginger juice.*

fish with sweet sauce

1. Mix together to make seasoning sauce:
   3 T sugar
   3 T vinegar
   4 T catsup
   1 T sherry
   1 t salt
   1 t sesame oil

   Set aside.

2. Heat in wok:
   2 T oil

3. Add and cook slowly:
   ½ C onion, diced
   4 Chinese mushrooms, soaked, diced

4. Add seasoning sauce.
   Cook, stirring until thick.

5. Add:
   3 T frozen peas and carrots, thawed

   Remove to warm bowl.

6. Mix together to make batter:
   1 egg
   ½ C flour
   1 t salt
   4½ T water

   Set aside.

7. Heat in wok to 375°:
   2 C oil

8. Dip into batter and deep-fry until golden:
   1 lb. sole, cut into 2 x ½'' pieces

   Drain and remove to serving platter.

9. To serve: pour warm sauce over fish.

hot and sour soup

1. Heat:

   4 C chicken broth

2. Add and stir in:

   4 oz. shoulder of veal, shredded

3. Add and cook for 3 minutes:

   4 Chinese mushrooms, soaked, shredded

   1 cake bean curd, shredded

   12 lily buds, soaked, cut into 1″ pieces

   1 T tree ears, soaked, shredded

   ¼ C bamboo shoots, shredded

4. Add and bring to a boil:

   2 t soy sauce

   1 t salt

   ½ t sugar

   2 T wine vinegar

   ½ t black pepper

5. Add, bring to a boil, and stir until thick:

   2 T cornstarch dissolved in 2 T water

6. Turn off flame and pour in:

   1 egg, slightly beaten

   Stir.

7. Pour into soup tureen.

8. Float on top:

   1 T sesame oil

9. Sprinkle over:

   Chinese parsley, minced, or scallion, minced

Chinese parsley is also known as fresh coriander or cilantro.

chicken egg drop soup

1. Bring to a boil:
   6 C chicken broth

2. Add and boil for 1 minute:
   ½ C water chestnuts, diced

3. Add, bring to a boil, and stir until thick:
   1½ T cornstarch dissolved in 2 T water

4. Add:
   ¼ C scallions, minced

5. Turn off flame and pour in:
   1 egg, slightly beaten

6. Mix and serve immediately.

wonton soup

1. Bring to a boil:
   5 C chicken broth

2. Place in an individual soup bowl:
   boiled wonton

3. Add hot chicken broth.

4. Garnish with a parbroiled, chopped green vegetable such as:
   spinach or bok choy

veal and leek soup

1. Bring to a boil:
   4 C chicken broth

2. Add and cook for 2 minutes:
   2 oz. shoulder of veal, shredded
   3 Chinese mushrooms, soaked, sliced
   1 leek, sliced
   1 t sherry

3. Add and cook for 2 minutes:
   2 oz. bamboo shoots, sliced
   2 oz. snow peas, cut into thirds
   ½ t salt

4. Bring to a boil again and add:
   2 drops sesame oil

   Serve hot.

veal and watercress soup

1. Bring to a boil:
   5 C chicken broth
   1 slice ginger root

   Remove ginger root.

2. Add, cover and simmer 10 minutes:
   4 oz. shoulder of veal, shredded
   ½ C celery, shredded

3. Add to stock and bring to boil:
   1 T sherry
   ½ T soy sauce
   2 scallions cut into 2″ pieces
   1 bunch watercress, cut into 2″ sections

   Serve hot.

taro rice soup

1. Bring to a boil:

   6 C chicken broth

   1 C short grain rice, uncooked

   Turn off heat and allow to stand for 30 minutes.

2. Heat in wok:

   2 T oil

3. Add to wok and stir-fry 3 minutes:

   2 lbs. taro, cut into 1″ cubes

   2 shallots

   ½ t salt

4. Add and cook for 2 minutes:

   1 cup chicken broth

5. Add the taro mixture to the broth and rice mixture, and cook for 15 minutes.

6. Heat in wok:

   1 T oil

7. Add to wok and stir-fry for 1 minute:

   ½ lb. Chinese long beans
   (or string beans)

   ½ t salt

8. Add the beans to the soup pot and cook for another 15 minutes.

   Serve hot.

This recipe is traditionally prepared with the Chinese vegetable, taro, a starchy, tuberous brown root, available fresh at an oriental market. One may very readily substitute sweet potato, white potato or butternut squash.

This soup is called **Congee** *and is traditionally served for breakfast or brunch. It's very hearty and thick. To thin it out, add more water while cooking.*

szechuen nutty chicken
kung po gai

1. Combine:
   2 T cornstarch
   1 egg white
   1 lb. chicken cutlets, cut into 2″ cubes

2. Heat in wok:
   1 T oil

3. Add and stir-fry for 2 minutes:
   1 clove garlic
   3 slices ginger root
   2 dried chili peppers, soaked, chopped
   1 green pepper, cut into 2″ pieces

4. Add coated chicken to wok. Stir-fry until chicken turns opaque.

5. Add to wok:
   3 T soy sauce
   1 T sherry
   2 t sugar
   2 t cornstarch dissolved in ½ C water

6. Cover and cook 5 minutes.

7. To serve, sprinkle with:
   ½ C unsalted peanuts, roasted

sweet and sour chicken

tiem shuen gai

1. Mix together to make batter:
   2 t baking powder
   1 C cold water
   1 C flour
   6 T oil
   1 t sherry

2. Dip into the batter:
   1 lb. chicken cutlets, cut into 1″ cubes

3. Heat in wok to 375°:
   2 C oil

4. Add and deep-fry the chicken until golden.

   Remove to a warm plate.

5. Heat in wok:
   2 T oil

6. Add to wok and stir-fry for 2 minutes:
   4 green peppers, cubed
   1 onion, cubed
   1 carrot, parbroiled, cubed
   1 C pineapple chunks, drained

7. Mix together to make seasoning sauce:
   6 T sugar
   2 T soy sauce
   1 T sherry
   2 T vinegar
   4 T catsup
   1 T cornstarch dissolved in ½ C water

8. Add seasoning sauce to vegetables in wok and simmer until bubbling, stirring constantly.

9. Add the deep-fried chicken and heat through.

   Serve immediately.

chicken with cucumbers

1. Heat in wok:

   1 T oil

2. Add and stir-fry for 1 minute:

   2 medium cucumbers, peeled, seeded, sliced thin

3. Add and stir-fry for 1 minute:

   1 t salt

   ½ t sugar

   Remove to plate, set aside.

4. Mix together:

   1 lb. chicken cutlets, cut into 1″ cubes

   1 T cornstarch

   1 T sherry

5. Heat in wok:

   2 T oil

6. Add to wok and stir-fry for 2 minutes:

   2 slices ginger root

7. Add marinated chicken cubes to wok and stir-fry until meat turns opaque.

8. Return cucumbers to wok and heat through.

   Serve immediately.

chicken with mushrooms

moo goo gai pien

1. Mix together to make marinade:

   1 t salt

   2 T sherry

   2 t cornstarch

   ⅛ t white pepper

2. Add to marinade for 10 minutes:

   ½ lb. chicken cutlets, cut into 1″ cubes

3. Heat in wok:

   1 T oil

4. Add to wok and stir-fry for 2 minutes:

   1 green pepper, cubed

   ½ C fresh mushrooms, cubed

   Remove and reserve.

5. Heat in wok:

   2 T oil

6. Add marinated chicken cubes to wok and stir-fry until opaque.

7. Add the reserved vegetables to wok and stir-fry for 1 minute.

8. Add 1 tablespoon water if mixture is too dry.

   Serve immediately.

chicken with hoisin sauce
hoy sin jheung gai

1. Mix together to make marinade:
   1 T soy sauce
   1 T sherry
   1 t cornstarch

2. Add to marinade:
   1 lb. chicken cutlets, cut into 1″ cubes

3. Heat in wok:
   1 T oil

4. Add to wok and stir-fry for 2 minutes:
   ½ C water chestnuts, diced
   ½ C fresh mushrooms, sliced
   1 C snow peas, cut into 1″ pieces
   ½ t salt

   Remove and set aside.

5. Heat in wok:
   3 T oil

6. Add marinated chicken to wok and stir-fry until chicken turns opaque.

7. Add and mix well:
   2 T hoisin sauce

8. Combine reserved vegetables with chicken and heat through.

9. To serve sprinkle with:
   ¼ C cashew nuts, roasted in a 350° oven for 10 minutes

chicken cantonese

1. Mix together to make marinade:
   ½ T cornstarch
   2 t sherry

2. Add to marinade for 10 minutes:
   **1½ lbs. chicken cutlets, cut into
   1½'' cubes**

3. Heat in wok:
   2 T oil

4. Add to wok and stir-fry for 1 minute:
   2 slices ginger root
   1 clove garlic, minced
   ¼ t salt
   ⅛ t pepper

5. Add and stir-fry until redness disappears:
   4 oz. ground beef

6. Add marinated chicken cubes and stir-fry until opaque.

7. Add and bring to a boil:
   ¾ C chicken broth
   1 T fermented black beans, minced

8. Mix together and stir into wok:
   **1½ T cornstarch dissolved in 2 T
   water**
   ½ t sugar
   1 t soy sauce

9. Add and stir in:
   1 egg, lightly beaten
   1 scallion, sliced thin

   Serve immediately.

fried chicken with walnuts

1. Mix together to make marinade:
   3 T cornstarch
   1 egg white
   2 T sherry
   ½ t salt

2. Add to marinade and set aside for 15 minutes:
   **12 oz. chicken cutlets, cut into
   2″ cubes**

3. Dredge marinated pieces of chicken in:
   **4 oz. walnuts, chopped into
   rice-size pieces**

4. Heat in wok to 350°:
   2 C oil

5. Deep-fry chicken until golden brown.

6. Serve with **Szechuen Pepper and Salt** for dipping.

szechuen pepper and salt

1. Mix together and stir in a wok over low heat for 2 minutes:
   1 T Szechuen peppercorns
   1 T salt
   Remove from heat and cool.

2. Grind the mixture very, very fine and then sift through a fine sieve. Discard outer shells.

This mixture will keep in a tightly covered bottle.

deep-fried chicken legs
gai jow

1. Marinate together for 2 hours:
   - **4 chicken legs**
   - **2 scallions, cut into 1″ pieces**
   - **2 slices ginger root, shredded**
   - **1 star anise, smashed**
   - **5 T soy sauce**
   - **1 T sherry**

2. Steam mixture for 30 minutes.

   Remove chicken and reserve 4 table-spoons cooking liquid.

3. Heat with reserved cooking liquid to make seasoning oil:
   - **2 T sesame oil**

   Keep warm.

4. Heat in wok to 375°:
   - **4 C oil**

5. Deep-fry chicken for 3 minutes until skin is crispy brown.

   Cut chicken into pieces with cleaver; arrange on serving platter.

6. Sprinkle over:
   - **1 T scallion, chopped**
   - **1 t Szechuen Pepper and Salt**

7. Pour warm seasoning oil mixture over.

   Serve.

lemon chicken I

1. Combine to make marinade:
   1 T soy sauce
   ½ t sesame oil
   ½ t salt
   1 T gin

2. Add to marinade:
   2½ lb. chicken, fryer or broiler, cut into 12 pieces

   Refrigerate 4 hours.

   Remove chicken and drain.

3. Coat chicken with:
   2 egg whites, beaten

4. Roll coated chicken in:
   flour

5. Heat in wok:
   1 T oil

6. Add to wok and stir-fry 2 minutes:
   1 carrot, par-boiled, sliced on diagonal
   1 green pepper, cut into 1″ cubes
   ¼ C pineapple chunks, drained
   Set aside.

7. Heat in wok to 375°:
   ½ inch oil

8. Deep-fry chicken in hot oil until golden.

   Remove to warm plate.

9. Combine in saucepan and simmer until thick, to make sauce:
   ⅓ C sugar
   ¼ C white vinegar
   ½ C chicken broth
   1 T cornstarch dissolved in 1 T water
   1 T lemon juice
   1 t grated lemon peel

10. Remove from heat and add:
    ½ oz. lemon extract

11. To serve, arrange chicken on a bed of:
    shredded lettuce

    Surround with stir-fried vegetables and fruit.

    Pour sauce over all.

lemon chicken II

1. Combine to make marinade:

   2 T soy sauce

   2 T vodka

2. Place into marinade:

   3½ lb. chicken, fryer or broiler, wiped dry

   Turn occasionally to coat skin.

   Refrigerate 4 hours.

3. Heat in wok to 375°:

   ½ inch oil

4. Deep-fry chicken until brown.

5. Place in roasting pan and bake, uncovered, in a 350° oven for 45 minutes.

6. Mix together, bring to a boil, and simmer until thick to make sauce:

   ¾ C sugar

   ½ C vinegar

   1 C chicken stock

   1 T cornstarch dissolved in 2 T water

   2 T lemon juice

   1 T grated lemon rind

   Remove from heat.

7. Add to sauce:

   ½ oz. lemon extract

8. Cut chicken into serving pieces and arrange on platter.

9. To serve: pour sauce over chicken, reserving some to pass in gravy boat.

   Garnish with lemon slices.

black satin chicken

1. Combine:
   1 T sherry
   ½ t salt
   1 t pepper

2. Rub seasoned sherry into:
   3 lb. chicken, pullet or roaster

3. Combine to make seasoning:
   4 slices ginger root
   3 scallions

   Place into cavity of bird.

4. Mix together and bring to a boil, to make cooking broth:
   ½ C soy sauce
   1 C water
   ½ C brown sugar
   4 Chinese mushrooms, soaked, shredded
   1 t sesame oil

5. Place chicken with filled cavity into broth, bring to boil, cover and simmer 45 minutes.

   Turn chicken often during this time to brown evenly. Remove.

6. Cut chicken into small sections and arrange on platter.

   Reserve cooking liquid.

7. Bring 1 cup reserved cooking liquid to a boil to make sauce.

8. Add:
   2 t cornstarch dissolved in 2 t water

9. Pour sauce over chicken.

10. To serve, garnish with:
    scallions, chopped

sesame chicken salad

jee ma gai

1. Boil 15 minutes:

   2 whole chicken breasts

   Cool and shred meat.

2. Combine to make seasoning sauce:

   1 T soy sauce
   ¼ t Chinese-style mustard
   1 t wine vinegar
   2 t sesame oil
   1 t sugar
   ½ t pepper

   Set aside.

3. Combine with chicken:

   2 stalks celery, blanched, shredded
   3 scallions, shredded

4. Add seasoning sauce to chicken mixture.

5. To serve sprinkle with:

   2 T toasted sesame seeds

chicken salad

1. Boil 15 minutes:

   1 whole chicken breast

   Cool and shred meat.

2. Soak in cold water for 10 minutes:

   2 oz. agar-agar

   Drain and cut into 2 inch pieces.

3. Par-boil:

   4 oz. bean sprouts

   Rinse with cold water.

4. Shred:

   1 carrot

5. Cut very thin:

   2 stalks celery

6. Mix together to form salad dressing:

   1 t salt
   2 T soy sauce
   2 T vinegar
   1 t sugar
   1 T sesame oil
   1 T hot oil

7. To serve: layer on serving plate the agar-agar, bean sprouts, celery, carrots and chicken. Pour the dressing over the salad 5 minutes before serving.

This is a fun dish to take to a picnic. Please carry dressing separately, combining with salad 5 minutes before serving.

szechuen chicken

1. Bring to a boil:
   2 qt. water
   2 slices ginger root
   1 scallion
   4 whole chicken breasts

2. Cover and boil 15 minutes.
   Turn off flame and allow chicken to cool in water.

   Remove.

3. Skin and bone chicken and pull into shreds.

4. Mix with chicken:
   4 C lettuce, shredded

5. Heat to just below the boiling point to make sauce:
   3 T oil
   ½ C scallion, chopped
   1 t Szecheun peppercorns, crushed
   ¼ t crushed red pepper
   2 ginger root slices, minced

   Remove from heat.

6. Add:
   2 T soy sauce
   1 T hoisin sauce
   1 clove garlic, minced
   1 T dark corn syrup

7. To serve: toss together.

The chicken and lettuce may be prepared ahead of time; place, covered, in the refrigerator. However, the sauce must be put on at the last minute.

steamed duck

jing opp

1. Combine to make seasoning sauce:

   1 T gin
   1 T soy sauce
   ½ t salt

2. Rub the seasoning sauce into the outside skin of:

   1 duck, 3-4 lbs.

   Put aside to dry.

3. Heat in wok to 375°:

   3 C cooking oil

4. In hot oil, deep-fry duck, continuously turning until golden brown.

   Drain.

5. Into cavity of bird place:

   3 cloves star anise
   2 Mandarin orange peels
   6 lotus seeds, cracked

   (It is not necessary to sew duck)

6. Combine in saucepot to make cooking liquid:

   2 T soy sauce
   2 C water

7. Place the duck into the saucepot with the liquid and simmer gently about 4 hours, rotating bird as it cooks.

   Test for doneness by pulling bones. The meat should slip off easily.

   Remove duck and reserve cooking liquid.

8. Cool duck enough to handle. Gently pull out all bones leaving the duck meat and skin in pieces as large as possible.

9. Line a 9″ bowl with:

   6 cabbage leaves, par-boiled

10. Place the skin and cooked duck meat into the lined bowl. Press down firmly.

11. Cover bowl with foil. Steam 10 minutes.

12. Invert onto serving platter.

13. Heat in wok:

    2 T oil

14. Add to wok and stir-fry 2 minutes:

    ½ Chinese cabbage, shredded

    ½ t salt

    1 t sugar

    Place around duck on serving platter.

15. Combine to make serving sauce:

    1 C hot reserved cooking liquid

    1 t cornstarch dissolved in 1 T water

    Bring to boil; stir to thicken.

16. Pour sauce over all.

Orange peel may be substituted for Mandarin orange peel. Almonds may be substituted for lotus seed.

peking duck
pei-ching-kao-ya

1. Combine to make warm syrup mixture:

   3 T honey

   2 T sherry

   1 T vinegar

   1 cup hot water

   Set aside.

2. Prepare:

   1 whole duck, 4-5 lbs.

   Wash under cold water and pat dry, inside and outside. Brush thoroughly with warm syrup mixture. Tie a string around the neck of the bird and hang it to dry in front of a fan for 3 hours. (It can also be hung in a drafty place and allowed to dry without the aid of a fan, for 10 hours.)

3. Place prepared duck on a rack in a roasting pan. Roast in 350° oven for ½ hour. Lower temperature to 275° and continue cooking for 1 hour more. Then raise temperature to 375° and continue cooking for ½ hour more. Turn duck 4 times during this roasting process. Remove duck from oven. Cool enough to handle. Remove the crisp skin from the entire duck, cut it into 2x3″ rectangles and arrange the skin on a warm serving platter. Remove all of the meat from the carcass, cutting it into pieces about ½″ thick by 2½″ long. Arrange on same serving platter. Place wings on platter.

Serve with **Sauce for Peking Duck, Scallion Brushes,** and **Peking Doilies.**

Traditionally, one places a pancake flat on one's plate, dips a scallion brush into the duck sauce and brushes the pancake with it. The scallion is placed in the middle of the pancake, with a piece of duck skin and a piece of duck meat. The pancake is folded over the filling, enclosing the filling, and then rolled into a cylindrical shape allowing it to be picked up and eaten with one's fingers.

sauce for peking duck

1. Heat in a small pot:
   1 T sesame oil

2. Add to oil, stir for 2 minutes until thick:
   3 T sweet bean sauce
   3 T sugar
   3 T water

   Remove to small serving bowl.

3. Serve with **Scallion Brushes.**

scallion brushes

Scallion brushes are prepared by taking 2 inch pieces of the white end of the scallion and repeatedly scoring the ends with a sharp knife, thus making a grid pattern to create a "bristle" effect.

peking doilies

*pancakes for peking duck
and moo sho roo*

1. Mix well together:

   ⅔ C boiling water

   3 C flour

   Set aside for 3 minutes.

2. Add:

   ⅓ C cold water

   Knead the mixture thoroughly until it is smooth, about 5 minutes. Cover the dough and let it rest 15 minutes.

3. Remove to lightly floured board and divide into 20 pieces.

   Form into 20 rounds, about 1'' in diameter and cover with a damp towel.

4. Remove one round, slightly flatten it. Spread vegetable shortening over top. Place a second slightly flattened round on top of this one. Roll the two out together to form one pancake 7 inches in diameter. Now separate the top piece from the underneath piece. You have achieved 2 thin pancakes. Repeat process until there are 20 **Peking Doilies.**

5. Cook in ungreased skillet, on one side only, until they become a parchment color — do not brown.

These pancakes can be made ahead and stored one day in the refrigerator, or they may be frozen. Pancakes should be steamed to bring to serving temperature.

moo sho roo

1. Simmer for 3 minutes:

   20 tiger lily buds, rinsed

   3 T tree ears, rinsed

   Drain and shred.

2. Heat in wok:

   2 T oil

3. Add and stir-fry for 1 minute:

   4 oz. chicken cutlets, shredded

4. Add tree ears and lily buds and cook 1 minute:

   2 t soy sauce

   1 C bamboo shoots, shredded

   ½ t sugar

   ¼ t salt

   Remove to a bowl.

5. Heat in wok:

   2 T oil

6. Scramble in hot oil until almost done:

   6 eggs, lightly beaten with ½ t sugar

7. Add reserved chicken mixture to egg mixture and cook for 1 minute:

   ¼ C chicken broth

   ½ C scallions, diced

Moo Sho Roo *may be eaten alone as is or served with* **Peking Doilies.** *Take a spoonful, place it in the center of the pancake, roll it up and eat it with your fingers.*

white rice

1. Combine and bring to a boil:
   1 C rice
   1¾ C water

2. Reduce heat, cover and cook 20 minutes. Do not peek.

3. Remove from heat, keep covered, and allow to rest for 20 minutes. Do not Peek.

4. Uncover and fluff up. Serve.

Steam to reheat rice.

fried rice

1. Heat in 7 inch fry pan:
   1 T oil

2. Pour in:
   2 beaten eggs

   Fry to form a pancake.

   Remove to cutting board, cool and shred. Set aside.

3. Heat in wok:
   2 T oil

4. Add to wok and stir-fry until opaque:
   ¼ lb. chicken cutlets, diced
   ¼ C scallion, diced
   1 C lettuce, shredded

5. Add and stir until completely hot:
   4 C cold, cooked rice
   3 T soy sauce

6. To serve: place rice on platter and garnish with shredded egg.

Rice must be cold to properly prepare this dish. Day old rice is best.

golden fried rice

1. Mix together:

   ½ lb. chicken cutlets, diced
   ½ t salt
   ⅛ t ginger powder
   ½ t sherry
   1 t cornstarch
   ½ egg white

2. Heat in wok:

   3 T oil

3. Add the chicken mixture to wok and stir-fry until opaque.

   Set aside.

4. Mix together:

   5 C cold cooked rice
   6 eggs, well beaten
   ½ t salt

5. Heat in wok:

   2 T oil

6. Add cold rice mixture to wok and stir-fry for 5 minutes:

   2 cloves garlic
   1 t salt

7. Then add and stir-fry for 1 minute:

   5 oz. frozen green peas, thawed
   ½ lb. smoked dark meat turkey, diced

8. Add chicken mixture and heat through.

   Serve.

fried rice stick
mei fun lok

1. Mix together:
   ½ lb. chicken cutlets, shredded
   3 T soy sauce
   1 t sugar
   1 T cornstarch

2. Heat in wok:
   3 T oil

3. Add marinated chicken to wok and stir-fry until meat turns opaque.

   Remove to warm plate.

4. Heat in wok:
   2 T oil

5. Add to wok and stir-fry for 2 minutes:
   1 lb. Chinese cabbage, shredded
   2 onions, sliced
   5 Chinese mushrooms, soaked, shredded
   ½ C dried lily buds, soaked

6. Add reserved chicken mixture and stir-fry gently until heated thru:
   1 lb. rice stick, soaked, drained

7. Add:
   1 C chicken broth

   Cover and cook 2 minutes.

8. Stir in:
   1 t salt

   Cook 3 minutes more.

   Serve immediately.

Rice stick is noodles made from rice flour. Soak before using.

vegetable and soft noodles
quar choy lo mein

1. Cook for 3 minutes in 2 qts. of boiling water:

   ½ lb. fresh egg noodles

   Drain.

2. Stir into cooked noodles:

   1 T oil

3. Place noodles in heavy skillet, over low heat, and brown slightly on one side; then turn over and brown on the other side. Remove to a warm serving platter.

4. Heat in wok:

   2 T oil

5. Add to wok and stir-fry for 3 minutes:

   ½ lb. Chinese cabbage, shredded

   ½ C bamboo shoots, shredded

   4 Chinese mushrooms, soaked, shredded

   ½ t salt

   1 T soy sauce

6. Add and bring to a boil:

   ½ C chicken broth

7. Add:

   2 t cornstarch dissolved in 2 T water

   Stir until thickened.

8. To serve: place brown noodles on a platter and top with vegetables. Garnish with:

   scallions, shredded

Number 9 spaghetti is a proper substitute for fresh egg noodles.

fried noodles

chow mein

1. Cook in boiling water for 5 minutes:

   10 oz. thin egg noodles

   Rinse in cold water and drain.

2. Add to noodles and mix well:

   1 T soy sauce
   1 T sesame oil

3. Heat in wok:

   4 T oil

4. Pour the noodle mixture into the wok and fry 3 minutes until the bottom is brown. Turn the noodles over.

5. Add around the edge of the wok:

   2 T oil

   Continue frying until the second side is brown. Remove to a serving platter.

6. Mix together:

   a total of 12 oz., chicken cutlets, gizzards and chicken liver, shredded
   2 T soy sauce
   1 T cornstarch

7. Heat in wok:

   4 T oil

8. Add to the wok and stir-fry the chicken mixture until the meat is cooked. Remove. Place on top of noodles.

9. Heat in wok:

   1 T oil

10. Add to wok and stir-fry for 1 minute:

    4 Chinese mushrooms, soaked, shredded
    4 oz. bamboo shoots, shredded

11. Add and mix well:

    8 oz. bean sprouts
    4 oz. spinach

12. Add:

    2 T soy sauce
    1 t salt
    ½ C chicken broth

13. Add and boil:

    2 t cornstarch dissolved in 2 T water

    Stir until thickened.

14. Add and stir in:

    3 scallions, cut into 2″ pieces
    ¼ C smoked dark meat turkey, shredded
    ½ t sesame oil

    Pour over noodle pancake.

fried noodle plate

1. Cook in boiling salted water for 5 minutes:

   5 oz. thin egg noodles

   Drain.

2. Add to noodles and mix well:

   1 T soy sauce
   1 T sesame oil

3. Heat in wok:

   4 T oil

4. Pour the noodle mixture into the wok and fry 3 minutes until the bottom is brown.

   Turn the noodles over.

5. Add around the edge of the wok:

   2 T oil

   Continue frying until the second side is brown.

   Remove to a large platter and chill.

6. Mix together to make marinade:

   2 T soy sauce
   1 t sugar
   1 T vinegar
   1 T sesame oil
   2 T peanut butter

7. Pour the marinade over:

   1 lb. cucumbers, peeled, seeded, shredded

   Refrigerate for 6 hours.

8. To assemble, place over the cold noodles:

   12 oz. smoked dark meat turkey, shredded

   Layer on the marinated cucumbers and the marinade.

9. Garnish with:

   scallions, chopped

This is a fun dish to take on a picnic or to a summer music festival. Of course, it complements any Chinese dinner, and becomes the star at a luncheon.

egg foo yung sub gum

1. Shred any combination of vegetables to make 2½ cups:

   bean sprouts
   celery, blanched
   mushrooms
   asparagus, blanched
   broccoli, blanched
   peas
   onions, blanched

2. Beat together and add to vegetables:

   6 eggs
   1 t salt
   2 t soy sauce
   1 t sherry

3. Heat in skillet:

   2 T oil

4. Drop ½ cup of egg mixture onto skillet to make 3'' omelet.

   Fry on one side, turn and brown lightly on the other side.

   Make one 3 inch omelet at a time.

   Remove and keep warm.

5. Serve with **Egg Foo Yung Sauce**.

egg foo yung sauce

1. Heat together:

   ¾ C chicken broth
   ½ t salt
   1 T soy sauce
   2 t sherry

2. Add and bring to boil:

   2 T cornstarch dissolved in 2 T water

   Stir to thicken.

broccoli, mushrooms and water chestnuts

guy lan mar tae dong goo

1. Heat in wok:
   2 T oil
   ½ t salt

2. Add to wok and stir-fry for 1 minute:
   1 bunch of broccoli, cut into 2″
      flowerettes, par-boiled for
      2 minutes

   Remove and reserve.

3. Heat in wok:
   2 T oil

4. Add to wok and stir-fry for 30 seconds:
   6 Chinese mushrooms, soaked,
      cubed, (reserve soaking liquid)
   10 water chestnuts, sliced

5. Add to wok:
   ½ C reserved mushroom liquid
   ½ C chicken broth
   1 t sherry
   1 T cornstarch
   2 T soy sauce

   Bring to a boil.

6. Add broccoli and heat through.

   Serve.

garlic spinach

1. Heat in wok:
   2 T oil

2. Add to wok and stir-fry for 30 seconds:
   3 cloves garlic, minced
   1 t salt

3. Add and stir-fry for 1 minute:
   1 lb. fresh spinach
   1 T sugar

   Serve hot.

The whole spinach leaf is used. It resembles a bird, the red tip representing the beak.

asparagus salad

1. Cook in 2 qts. of boiling water for 2 minutes:

   2 lbs. fresh asparagus, cut into 1½'' pieces

2. Rinse with cold water and drain. Pat dry.

3. Combine to make seasoning sauce:

   4 t soy sauce

   1 t sugar

   1 t sesame oil

4. Pour over asparagus, chill and serve.

green beans

chow dow jai

1. Heat in wok:

   2 T oil

2. Add and stir-fry for 2 minutes:

   2 cloves garlic, crushed

   1 t salt

   1 lb. tender green beans cut into 1'' pieces

3. Add to wok and cook covered for 2 minutes:

   ½ C water

   2 t soy sauce

   Remove to a platter and cool.

4. To serve, sprinkle with:

   ¾ C toasted, slivered almonds

beef, broccoli in black bean sauce

guy lon dow see

1. Mix together and set aside:
    **1 lb. shoulder steak, sliced thin, cut
       into 2″ pieces**
    2 T soy sauce
    2 T cornstarch
    1 T sherry
    1 t sugar

2. Place in bowl, cover with boiling water
   and allow to stand 2 minutes:
    **1 bunch broccoli, broken into 2″
       flowerettes**

   Cool immediately by immersing in cold
   water.

   Drain well.

3. Heat in wok:
    2 T oil
    ½ t salt

4. Add broccoli to wok and stir-fry for 2
   minutes.

   Remove to warm plate.

5. Heat in wok:
    3 T oil

6. Add to wok and stir-fry for 1 minute:
    1 slice ginger root
    2 cloves garlic, crushed

7. Add the meat mixture.

   Stir-fry until redness disappears.

8. Add to wok and stir-fry until thickened:
    2 T fermented black beans, minced
    ½ C chicken broth

9. Add the broccoli and heat through.

   Remove to platter and serve.

beef with snow peas
soot dow ngow

1. Soak together for 10 minutes:
   2 scallions, crushed
   3 slices ginger root, crushed
   ½ t sherry
   4 T cold water

2. Add to this mixture and marinate for 1 hour:
   ¼ t pepper
   1 T soy sauce
   1 T flour
   1 T cornstarch
   1 lb. shoulder steak, cut ¼″ thick, sliced into 1½″ pieces

3. Heat in wok to 375°:
   3 C oil

4. Deep-fry marinated beef for 30 seconds. Remove, drain and set aside.

5. In a sauce pot heat:
   1 T oil

6. Add and bring to a boil:
   1½ T soy sauce
   1 T catsup
   1 T hot oil
   2 T sugar
   1 t cornstarch
   3 T water

   Turn off heat.

7. Add cooked beef.

8. Add and mix well:
   1 T scallion, chopped

   Remove to serving platter.

9. Heat in wok:
   2 T oil
   ½ t salt

10. Add to wok and stir-fry for 2 minutes:
    ½ lb. snow peas

11. To serve: arrange snow peas around steak.

steak kew

1. Heat in wok:
   ½ T oil
   ½ t salt

2. Add to wok and stir-fry for 3 minutes on each side:
   1 boneless rib eye steak, cut ¾'' thick

3. Remove from pan and cut into 1'' cubes.

4. Heat in wok:
   1 T oil

5. Add to wok and stir-fry 2 minutes:
   1½ C bok choy, shredded
   ¼ C water chestnuts, sliced
   ¼ C bamboo shoots, sliced
   ¼ C Chinese mushrooms, soaked, sliced
   ¼ C snow peas, cut into 1'' pieces
   1 t salt

6. Add and cook covered for 2 minutes:
   ½ C chicken broth

7. Add cubed steak to wok, and cook for 1 minute more, stirring constantly:
   1 T cornstarch dissolved in
      2 T water
   ½ t sugar
   ⅛ t pepper

Serve at once.

This recipe may be doubled.

beef, snow peas and baby corn
quar choy ngow chow

1. Mix together to make seasoning sauce:
   2 T soy sauce
   2 T cornstarch
   1 T sherry
   1 t sugar
   1 T oil

2. Add to the seasoning sauce and set aside:
   1 lb. shoulder steak, sliced thin, cut into 2″ pieces

3. Heat in wok:
   2 T oil

4. Add to wok and stir-fry for 1 minute:
   ½ t salt
   ¼ lb. snow peas, blanched, rinsed in cold water
   4 oz. baby corn, cut in half, lengthwise

   Remove to warm plate.

5. Heat in wok:
   3 T oil

6. Add to wok and stir-fry for 1 minute:
   1 slice ginger root
   2 cloves garlic

7. Add the meat and the seasoning sauce to wok and stir-fry until redness disappears.

8. Add and stir until sauce thickens:
   ½ C chicken broth

9. Return snow peas and baby corn to wok and heat through.

   Serve immediately.

Baby corn is found canned at an oriental food market.

beef with string beans

dow jai ngow

1. Combine to make marinade:
   - **2 T cornstarch**
   - **2 T soy sauce**
   - **1 T sherry**
   - **½ t sugar**

2. Add to marinade for 10 minutes:
   - **1 lb. shoulder steak, sliced thin, cut into 2 inch pieces**

3. Heat in wok:
   - **1 T oil**

4. Add to wok and stir-fry for 2 minutes:
   - **1 C string beans, blanched, cut into thirds**

   Remove and set aside.

5. Heat in wok:
   - **3 T oil**

6. Add to wok and stir-fry for 1 minute:
   - **4 slices ginger root**

7. Add beef mixture and stir-fry until redness disappears.

8. Add string beans.

   Remove ginger root.

9. Mix well and serve at once.

red simmered beef

hoong shu

1. Heat in wok:

   2 T oil

2. Sear in hot oil:

   2 lbs. boneless beef for stewing, cut into 1″ cubes

3. Add and bring to a boil:

   ½ C sherry
   ¼ C soy sauce
   1 T sugar
   1 C water
   1 star anise
   2 slices ginger root
   2 scallions, cut into 2″ pieces

4. Cover, reduce heat and simmer 1 hour.

Meat which is cooked in soy sauce for a long time is termed red simmering, although there is no true red color.

It aids the hostess in that it can be done early the same day and then reheated, done the day before and reheated, or frozen well in advance. It frees the hostess to concentrate on stir-fry dishes.

pearl meat balls
lor mei jing ngow yuk

1. Rinse in cold water until the water is clear:

   ½ C glutinous rice

2. Cover with cold water; set aside 2 hours. Drain and remove to a sheet of wax paper.

3. Mix together:

   ¼ C Chinese mushrooms, soaked, minced
   ¼ C water chestnuts, minced
   1 slice ginger root, minced
   1 scallion, minced
   1 egg
   1 T cornstarch
   1 T soy sauce
   1 t sherry
   1 t salt

4. Add, mixing together lightly but thoroughly:

   ½ lb. ground veal
   ½ lb. ground beef

5. Form the mixture into 1 inch balls.

   Roll the balls in the rice.

   Place on oven-proof serving dish.

6. Steam over high heat for 30 minutes.

7. Serve with mustard and soy sauce.

Glutinous rice is obtained at an oriental market. It is short-grained, opaque and pearly white. It is sometimes referred to as sweet rice.

steamed meat with taro
jing ngow woo tow

1. Mix together to make marinade:

   ½ t salt

   1½ t sesame oil

   1 T sherry

   1 T sugar

   ⅛ t five spice powder

   2 scallions, chopped

   3 slices ginger root

   3 T soy sauce

2. Add to the marinade:

   12 oz. shoulder steak, sliced ⅛″ thick, cut into 2″ pieces

   12 oz. taro, peeled, then washed and cut into thin 2″ slices

   Set aside for 1 hour.

   Remove to plate, reserve marinade.

3. Dredge marinated meat in:

   1 C Rice Powder

   Reserve leftover rice powder.

4. Place on oven-proof serving platter in one layer:

   lettuce leaves

5. Layer on the marinated taro.

6. Sprinkle with:

   ½ t salt

7. Layer the meat over.

8. Mix together remaining rice powder and remaining marinade.

   Pour over top of meat.

9. Steam over high heat for 1½ hours.

This recipe is traditionally prepared with the Chinese vegetable, taro, a starchy, tuberous brown root, available fresh at an oriental market. One may readily substitute sweet potato, white potato or butternut squash.

Rice powder may be purchased or prepared.

rice powder

1. Soak together for 1 hour:

   1 C uncooked rice

   2 C hot water

   Drain and remove to board.

2. Roll with rolling pin to powdered state.

stuffed cucumber
young min

1. Mix together thoroughly:

   4 oz. ground veal
   1 T bamboo shoots, minced
   1 T water chestnuts, minced
   1 scallion, minced
   1 T ginger root, minced
   1 T soy sauce
   ½ t sugar
   1 T sherry

2. Stuff this mixture into:

   1 large cucumber, cut into 4 equal pieces, then seeded to create hollow cylinders

3. Sprinkle over the top and bottoms of stuffed cucumber:

   1 T cornstarch

4. Heat in wok:

   2 T oil

5. Sear cucumbers in hot oil, meat side down, for 2 minutes. Turn over and sear the other side.

6. Mix together:

   ½ C chicken broth
   2 t soy sauce
   1 t sherry
   ¼ t salt

7. Pour over cucumbers and cook, covered, over low heat, for 20 minutes.

8. Add:

   1 t cornstarch dissolved in 1 t water

   Boil, mixing, until thick.

   Serve.

This recipe can also be used to stuff tomatoes, green pepper and the Chinese vegetable, bitter cucumber.

manderin fruit compote

1. Mix together:

    1 ripe pineapple, cubed
    1 pt. strawberries, halved
  11 oz. can lechee fruits, drained
  11 oz. can mandarin oranges, drained
    4 oz. preserved kumquats, seeded, halved
 1½ T kumquat syrup
    2 bananas, sliced on the diagonal
   ¾ C white rum
    2 T candied ginger, minced

Steep overnight.

2. To serve, spoon into champagne glasses and top with:

    shredded coconut

Add a miniature Chinese umbrella.

chinese almond gelatin

1. Mix together in a pot:
   1 oz. agar-agar, rinsed
   5 C cold water

   Cook over medium heat for 15 minutes.

2. Add to the pot and blend in well:
   2 T sugar

   Strain into a big bowl.

3. Add to bowl and stir briskly until thoroughly blended:
   5 T liquid non-dairy creamer
   1 T almond extract

4. Ladle this mixture into:
   melon halves

   Refrigerate for 2 hours.

5. Garnish with:
   a pineapple ring
   a marachino cherry.

almond float

1. Ladle into a greased 9x9" pan:
   unset Chinese Almond Gelatin

   Refrigerate for 2 hours.

2. Mix together to make sweetened water:
   4 C hot water
   1 C superfine sugar
   1 t almond extract

   Cool.

3. To serve: fill a large crystal bowl with the sweetened water. Float in it the almond gelatin, which has been cut into the traditional diamond shaped pieces.

4. Garnish with:
   manderin orange segments
   pineapple chunks
   lichee fruit

little chinese almond cakes

1. Cut in together:
   - ¼ C shortening
   - ¼ C margarine
   - 1 C flour

2. Work in, using hands:
   - ½ t salt
   - 6 T sugar
   - 2 T almond extract

3. Shape into long roll, 1 inch in diameter.

   Wrap in waxed paper.

   Chill 1 hour.

4. Cut roll into 24 slices.

   Place 1 inch apart on ungreased cookie sheet.

5. Brush slices with:
   - 1 egg mixed with 1 T water

6. Press on top of each cookie:
   - 1 blanched almond half

7. Bake in a 375° oven for 5-8 minutes until golden.

lemon cloud

1. Soften:

    ½ gallon lemon ice

2. Add:

    9½ oz. jar kumquats, drained, seeded, chopped

    3 oz. candied ginger, chopped

3. Refreeze.

4. Serve with cookies.

ginger slices

1. Cream together:

    1 C margarine

    1 C sugar

2. Add:

    ½ C molasses

    1 T ground ginger

    1¼ t cinnamon

    ½ t cloves

    1 t baking soda

    2 C almonds, slivered

3. Stir in:

    3¼ C flour

4. Shape dough into 5 long rolls 1 inch in diameter.

    Chill.

5. Cut rolls into 60 slices.

    Place 1 inch apart on lightly greased cookie sheet.

6. Bake in a 350° oven for 8-10 minutes.

peking dust

1. To 2 cups boiling water, add:

   1 C shelled pecans

   Boil 1 minute. Drain.

2. Add:

   ½ C sugar

   Mix well to coat pecans.

   Spread nuts on a plate to dry for 30 minutes.

3. Heat in wok to 375°:

   1 C oil

4. In hot oil, deep-fry the dried pecans until golden brown.

   Place on an oiled dish to dry.

5. Boil for 40 minutes:

   1 lb. Italian chestnuts, scored

   Drain, cool, and shell.

6. Grind chestnuts and mix with:

   1 T brown sugar

   Set aside.

7. Whip together until stiff:

   16 oz. non-dairy whipping cream
   1 t almond extract

8. To serve: mound whipped non-dairy whipping cream on a serving dish. Cover mound with chestnut mixture and surround it with fried pecans.

Other nuts may be fried in the same manner.

fortune cookies

1. Sift together:
   - ¼ C cake flour
   - 2 T sugar
   - 1 T cornstarch
   - ⅛ t salt

2. Add and stir until smooth:
   - 2 T oil
   - 1 egg white

3. Add and mix well:
   - 1 T water

4. Pour 1 tablespoon batter onto lightly greased skillet, to make 3½ inch round. Cook over low heat for 4 minutes. Turn with a wide spatula and cook 1 minute more.

   Work quickly. Put cookie on a pot holder and place the paper fortune in the center. Fold cookie in half and then bring cookie points together. Repeat 8 times.

5. Cool cookies in muffin tin.

This recipe may be doubled.

When a fool holds his tongue, he too is thought clever.   PROVERBS

If you don't run so far, the way back will be shorter.   MIDRASH

He who advertises his name, loses it.   HILLEL

If you grease the wheels, you can ride.   SHOLEM ALEICHEM

In business, everything depends on aid from heaven.   TALMUD

The greatest charity is to enable the poor to earn a living.   TALMUD

If you don't respect your parents, your child will not respect you.   MAIMONIDES

Be the master of your will, and the slave of your conscience.   HASIDIC SAYING

Include yourself in any reproof.   NACHMAN OF BRATSLAV

The man who spares the rod hates his son.   PROVERBS

Both right and wrong are the work of our hands.   PSALMS OF SOLOMON

Evil is sweet in the beginning but bitter in the end.   TALMUD

If a man carries his own lantern, he need not fear darkness.   HASIDIC SAYING

Obeying out of love is better than obeying out of fear.   RASHI

To pull a friend out of the mire, don't hesitate to get dirty.   BAAL SHEM TOV

Of the making of books, there is no end.   ECCLESIASTES

index